SEMITIC INFLUENCE IN HELLENIC MYTHOLOGY

SEMITIC INFLUENCE IN HELLENIC MYTHOLOGY

WITH SPECIAL REFERENCE TO THE RECENT MYTHOLOGICAL WORKS OF THE RT. HON. PROF. F. MAX MÜLLER AND MR. ANDREW LANG

BY

ROBERT BROWN, Jun., f.s.a., m.r.a.s.

' The truth can be discovered by careful research. We must not despair of truth.'
LANG.

Wipf & Stock
PUBLISHERS
Eugene, Oregon

Wipf and Stock Publishers
199 W 8th Ave, Suite 3
Eugene, OR 97401

Semitic Influence in Hellenic Mythology
With Special Reference to the Recent Mythological Works
of the Rt. Hon. Prof. F. Max Müller and Mr. Andrew Lang
By Brown, Robert
ISBN: 1-59752-625-8
Publication date 4/11/2006
Previously published by Williams and Norgate, 1898

PREFACE

THE leaders in England of two schools of mythology, based mainly in the one case on Aryan linguistics and in the other on anthropology, have recently published their revised, and probably final, conclusions. The time, therefore, seems opportune for a statement of the principles of a third School, which, for present purposes, I may style the Aryo-Semitic. Its members, whilst paying every respect to the system of Aryan philology, and fully recognizing the vast results that have sprung from the scientific application of Aryan linguistics, are nevertheless of opinion that the Aryanists have been unable to explain Hellenic mythology and Hellenic archaic history as a whole, because they have almost wholly ignored or denied the existence of that great mass of Semitic influence, which the Aryo-Semitic School hold is to be found throughout the length and breadth of Hellas. This latter School, moreover, is in entire sympathy with the researches of anthropology in general, and of folklore in particular. They welcome light from any quarter, but they more especially direct attention to that important influence, becoming clearer to us almost every year, which the Valleys of the Euphrates and of the Nile, and the populations of Syria and of Asia Minor have exercised upon the Greek mind.   Long-established theories, whatever great names they may claim in their support, must, perforce, give way to facts. Everything is a question of evidence, but in each case the best evidence attainable should be procured. It will never do, with Mr. Herbert Spencer, to first cut and dry your theory, and then to send out gleaners to gather facts in its support.

At present in England there is a kind of lazy feeling in the air; and, in the department of literature, this makes itself felt by the wish to be acquainted with the latest results of research without trouble. The State has decided that education is necessary; and the want of it is now felt, except in the case of persons of high social position, to be somewhat disgraceful.   Knowledge, people admit, is delightful; but then its acquisition is so painful.   This wish to be up to date with very little effort, naturally drives men to sit at the feet of smart Gamaliels, who, in a few piquant pages, purport to demolish the conclusions at which sages of European fame may have arrived after half a century of toil; and to replace their exploded teachings by another gospel of most superior brand.   Let us not be too sure about such alleged rapid gains. Great results generally arise from great efforts; just as good workmanship is almost universally costly. Many men are highly educated in a way. But that is not enough; to impart real benefit, they must also be possessed of refined common sense. Do not let us over-estimate the advantages conferred by mere education as ordinarily understood. Its results mainly depend upon the inherent character of the soil into which it falls. Thus, education can never make fools wise; but it can undoubtedly bestow upon them a larger area for the exercise of their folly.

I leave with confidence the following pages to the careful consideration of the reader, whether he chance to be critic, professional reviewer, scholar Classical or Oriental, anthropologist, folklorist, or honest man in the street who wishes to know something about these matters. I only ask him, whoever he may be, to weigh the questions well; and, without fear or favour, to give a true verdict according to the evidence.

In the spelling of names, I generally adopt the original forms, because they are the most correct. Severe logical uniformity in this matter is not at present attainable. A correct practice is, however, steadily gaining ground, notwithstanding divers violent protests on the part of some of those who think that Time can consecrate error and canonise stupidity.

The illustration on the cover, representing Hêraklês and the Stymphalian Birds, as shown on a Gem at Florence, is taken from Smith's *Smaller Classical Dictionary*, by the kind permission of Mr. John Murray.

BARTON-ON-HUMBER:
   March, 1898.

CONTENTS

PART I.

PROFESSOR MAX MÜLLER'S LAST PRONOUNCEMENT ON MYTHOLOGY.

PART II.

MR. LANG'S LATEST ATTACK UPON PROFESSOR MÜLLER.

PART III.

THE ARYO-SEMITIC SCHOOL OF HELLENIC MYTHOLOGISTS

ABBREVIATIONS

C. = Rt. Hon. Prof. Max Müller, *Contributions to the Science of Mythology* (1897).

M. M. = Mr. Andrew Lang, *Modern Mythology* (1897).

W. A. I. = *Cuneiform Inscriptions of Western Asia*, Vols. I.-V. (Published by the Trustees of the British Museum).

K. = *Kouyunjik Collection of Cuneiform Tablets* (British Museum).

Ak. = Akkadian.

Ar. = Arabic.

As. = Assyrian.

Bab. = Babylonian.

Et. = Etruscan.

Ph. = Phoenician.

Sk. = Sanskrit.

Sum. = Sumerian.

SEMITIC INFLUENCE IN HELLENIC MYTHOLOGY

PART I

PROFESSOR MAX MÜLLER'S LAST PRONOUNCEMENT ON MYTHOLOGY

I. Prof. Müller's Achievements

RIPE in years and rich in honours Prof. Max Müller
has now completed his self-imposed and formidable
task of giving to the world his facts and theories
respecting the four sciences of Language, Religion,
Thought and Mythology. And if the old soldier of
seventy-three finds, to our universal regret, that his
eye grows somewhat dim and his natural force abates
(Vide *C.* p. xxvi), he has not to grieve, with the
beautiful Kallikratês (Vide Herod. ix. 72), that he
must pass to the great silence without having lifted
his arm against the enemy or done deed worthy of
him. For, though ever gentle in the tourney, and
specially objecting to that keen personal controversy
which so easily degenerates into unmannerly
bickerings, Prof. Müller, however we may differ
with him in detail, has done many a doughty deed,
illumined many a dark spot, vastly widened the
bounds of our knowledge, placed his views before
the world in due completeness, and, if the translation
of the *Rig-Veda* be an achievement reserved for the

1

twentieth century, sung his song to the last stanza. And it is upon his great contributions to human knowledge and to human thought, and not merely upon an elegant and luminous style,—as Mr. Andrew Lang (*M. M.* p. 200) suggests, in a compliment which, however well meant, closely borders upon an insult,—that Prof. Müller's permanent fame will securely rest.

II. General Plan of the 'Contributions to the Science of Mythology'

These two goodly volumes, containing 900 pages, are divided into a Preface and six chapters, the first of which is a Retrospect, whilst the others severally treat of the Problems and Methods of the Science of Mythology, of the Analogical and Psychological Schools of Comparative Mythology, of Phonetics, and, lastly, of Vedic Mythology. In the Preface the Professor shows that, as a matter of fact, his method and general principles are not obsolete and bygone, as has of late been sometimes asserted in England. He is no solitary Athanasius, but has numerous very powerful fellow-workers, disciples, and allies, alike in Europe and in America. This, of course, is well known to scholars, but is frequently forgotten by those who draw their inspiration from the latest article in some English magazine. Thus, Mr. Andrew Lang remarks:—

'Mr. Max Müller's ideas, in various modifications, are doubtless still the most prevalent of any. The anthropological method has hardly touched, I think, the learned contributors to Roscher's excellent mythological Lexicon.'

On this I may observe that, whilst the scientific mind of Germany, as of course, welcomes all sober research, anthropological or otherwise, it is dead against the methods of the ' untutored anthropologist,' and for reasons which will clearly appear in these pages.

Alluding to a recent phase of literary opinion in England, Prof. Müller says :—

' If, as happens sometimes, the same critic is on the staff of many papers, and has to supply copy every day, every week, or every month, the broken rays of one brilliant star may produce the dazzling impression of many independent lights, and there has been of late such a galaxy of sparkling articles on Comparative Mythology and Folklore, that even those who are themselves opposed to this new science, have at last expressed their disapproval of the "journalistic mist " that has been raised, and that threatens to obscure the real problems of the Science of Mythology ' (C. p. vii).

He concludes his Preface with the following clear and large-hearted expression of his standpoint :—

' Whoever recognizes in mythology the last traces of [what we now call] a poetical conception of the solemn drama of nature, is on our side, and whatever the grammar and literature may be which he chooses for his own special study, whether those of Babylon or Egypt, of Lets or Fins, of Maoris or Mincoupies or Mincopies, if he can draw from them any contributions towards the elucidation of our ancient Aryan myths, he will be welcomed as a useful ally and as a worthy fellow-labourer ' (Ib. p. xxviii).

1 *

III. Study of Savage Tribes

Whilst thus welcoming all sound research, whether linguistic, mythological or anthropological, Prof. Müller urges that the study of the beliefs and customs of savages should be made with great care and caution ; and that it is most desirable that the investigator should, at all events to some extent, master the language of those about whom he is going to write.   He observes :—

' I can quite understand the strong prejudice which scholars feel against the purely dilettante work of certain ethnologists who write about the customs and myths of people whose language they do not understand' (*Ib.* p. 24).

This eminently reasonable opinion has been received with a grimace in certain quarters. Nor is the cause far to seek ; for it is vastly easier to compare the statements of a dozen books than to learn a single foreign language.

Innumerable mistakes have been made respecting the beliefs of savages, partly through the carelessness of investigators, but largely through misapprehensions arising from linguistic ignorance.   The same expressions, the same words, the same sounds, constantly mean very different things to different people.

IV. The Original Aryan Unity

As the now scattered branches of the Indo-European race were once a united family possessed of a single language (Proto-Aryan), Prof. Müller holds that, prior to their separation, they had 'not only common words ($\mu\hat{v}\theta o\iota$), but likewise common myths ($\mu\hat{v}\theta o\iota$.' *Ib.* p. 21).   The contrary proposition is almost unthinkable. The dwellers in Yorkshire, Greece, Mangaia, or anywhere else, have always had both. If anything further is required in support of so obvious a truth, let us quote the high authority of Mr. Lang, who, speaking of the 'Saranyu-Erinnys myth,' observes :—

'Why the story occurred both in Greece and India, I protest that I cannot pretend to explain, except on the hypothesis that the ancestors of Greek and Vedic peoples once dwelt together, had a common stock of savage fables, and a common or kindred language. After their dispersion, the fables admitted discrepancies, as stories in oral circulation occasionally do' (*M. M.* p. 69).

Just so. Prof. Müller next holds :—

'That what we call the gods of mythology were chiefly the agents supposed to exist behind the great phenomena of nature' (*C.* p. 21).

I confess I find little or no difference amongst investigators upon this point. Some, indeed, may give more prominence to the Dawn-spirit, 'other some' to the Corn-spirit, so beloved by Mannhardt and Mr. J. G. Frazer. But that does not touch the principle. If we take away from the mind of the men of archaic times 'the great phenomena of nature,' and all agents supposed to be connected with them, there is not much left for the Archaics to make gods out of. They would almost have been compelled to fall back on Mr. Herbert Spencer's ancestor-worship. But it is agreed on all sides that this theory practically involves a 'hysteron proteron' and cannot be accepted (Vide *C.* 3, 154-5 ; *M. M.* p. 126, note).

Prof. Müller next holds :—

'That the names of some of these gods and heroes, common to some or to all the branches of the Aryan family of speech, and therefore much older than the Vedic or Homeric periods, constitute the most ancient and the most important material on which students of [Aryan] mythology have to work' (*C.* p. 21).

That there should be some such god- and hero-names is practically as certain as that existing Aryan dialects possess numerous common ordinary words in variant forms. But, considering the lapse of time, and the special influences which affect proper names, it is a fair question to ask, Can we now identify and successfully compare any or many of these? This is, of course, a matter of evidence; and the evidence in support of identification is two-fold (1) That based upon linguistics—phonetic laws; and (2) That based upon similarity of concept and treatment in detail of any two mythic personages. It is not asserted that linguistics alone are to be relied upon. Lastly, as there is admittedly a Hyponoia (= Undercurrent of meaning) in mythology, Prof. Müller holds :—

'That the best solvent of the old riddles of mythology is to be found in an etymological analysis of the names of gods and goddesses, heroes and heroines' (*Ib.* p. 21).

The meaning of the name is obviously of very great importance in any attempt to explain a mythic personage. But although the meanings of vast numbers of ordinary words and of proper names are known, yet some of both kinds continue to defy all attempts at solution. The etymology of others, again, is doubtful.

V.   Vedic-Sanscrit and Greek Equations

The following instances give some of Prof. Müller's identifications of Vedic and Greek mythic personages, based upon the principles before mentioned, and maintained by him after considering carefully various objections urged by different critic-scholars :—

Sk. Ahanâ = Gk. Athêna ; Sk. Bhura*n*yu = Gk. Phorôneus; Sk. Dyaushpitar = Gk. Zeus-πατήρ (= Lat. Ju-piter) ; Sk. Sara*n*yu = Gk. Erînys ; Sk. Sârvara = Gk. Kerberos ; Sk. Ushas = Gk. Êôs ; Sk. Varuna = Gk. Ouranos ; Sk. Vivasvân = Gk. Iasiôn (*i.e.*, ΓιϜάσϜον).

To such comparisons two objections have been made. The first is that of certain scholars ; nearly all these equations, they say, violate some phonetic law, and are therefore impossible. The second objection is that urged by Mr. Lang as protagonist and on behalf of a certain class of anthropological mythologists. They say, in effect, We know nothing, and care very little, about linguistics. But we observe that the philological experts often differ in opinion. As, in the abstract, and, for aught we know, the opinion of Prof. A. is just as good as that of Dr. B., it will be wise to accept neither view ; and, further, to conclude that both opinions are alike worthless. This second objection I shall deal with subsequently (Vide *inf.* p. 35).

VI.   Instance of a Phonetic Objection

Another well-known equation, Sk. Sârameya-s = Gk. Hermeias, was first made by Kuhn. ' This

discovery,' says Prof. Müller, ' marked a new starting
point in our studies, and it was so brilliant and
so convincing that for a time it took even classical
scholars by storm. Afterwards followed a reaction.
Every kind of phonetic difficulty was raised, but
every objection was met, and after Benfey's exhaustive
paper on Hermes, Mînos, and Tartaros, the phonetic
objectors were finally silenced ' (*C.* p. 676). Not
' finally.' The persecution of this much-tried
equation soon recommenced. Mr. L. R. Farnell,
on the strength of ' information received ' from his
' friend Professor Macdonell,' thus confidently
expresses himself :—

' The theory that Sārameyá-s is to be identified
with Ἑρμείας founders on the first vowel : the Greek
equivalent should be Ἡρεμει-ος ' (*Cults of the Greek
States*, i. 3, note).

Is this so? Fick, in his list of the words of the
Aryan ' Grundsprache ' (*Wörterbuch*, i. 227), gives
the root *sar*, meaning primarily ' to go,' and equates
Sk. *sar-ma*, Gk. ὁρ-μή (' impetus '). From the root
sar spring Sk. *sar-aní* (' a path '), Sar-anyú
(' Morning-wind '), Saramâ, 'and her offspring
Sârameya' (*C.* i. 370. Note Prof. Müller's argument
in loc.). And, as Prof. Müller notes from Fick
(*Griech. Personennamen*, p. 467), ' the elision of the
middle vowel is justified by such an example as
Harpyiae-Arepyiae. The connexion between Hermês,
the Gk. ὁρμάω, and Sk. words compounded with the
root *sar*, is also supported by Scherer in ' Roscher's
excellent Lexicon ' (Vide *sup.* p. 2). Have, then,
Kuhn, Benfey, Fick, Scherer, Roscher, and
Prof. Müller all ' foundered ' ' on the first vowel '?
I beg leave to doubt. And, again, if we were

compelled to accept such a Gk. form as *Hêre-meios* (or -*meias*. Cf. the form *Hermeas, Il.* v. 390), why should it not be, abraded into *Her*-meias, just as *Hêra*-kles reappears as *Her*-cules? Let it not be supposed that I am inclined to undervalue the opinion of Prof. Macdonell. I learn from Mr. Lang (*M. M.* p. 201) that the Professor is 'the representative of the historic house of Lochgarry'; and I should as soon think of speaking disrespectfully of the equator. But when a point of law is decided by, say nine to three of the Judges, reasonable people don't, as a rule, continue to doubt about it. They regard the question as settled. According to Prof. Macdonell, only one of these philological equations 'between names of Greek and Vedic gods,' 'can be said to be beyond the range of doubt.' Well, well; people may doubt about almost anything. 'What is history but a fable agreed upon?' It has recently been strenuously and learnedly argued that the Gunpowder Plot was 'a put-up job' by the Earl of Salisbury. Prof. Müller, as of course, admits an absence of mathematical certainty in linguistic research. But, far from repining, let us be thankful for small mercies from Prof. Macdonell. One of these equations, it seems, is above suspicion. All hail, Calpurnia ! This fact may imply more than the Professor reckons on.

VII. Application of Phonetic Rules to Proper Names

But here a further question arises, *i.e.,* Do general phonetic rules 'apply with equal force to proper names, more particularly to the names of mythological gods and heroes?' (*C.* p. 297). Curtius said yes; Benfey, Prof. Victor Henry, Prof. Müller and others

say no. Prof. Müller, with a courageous love of
truth, ingenuously confesses :—' I formerly agreed
with Curtius' (*Ib.* p. 387); 'in former years I was
myself one of the straitest sect of phonetic pharisees.
But facts are facts, and one must live and learn'
(*Ib.* p. 425). 'As long as our facts cannot be
denied, our deductions will have to be accepted'
(*Ib.* p. 298).

And what are these facts? Why, that, from a
multitude of causes, proper names, especially those
'which have lost their etymological clearness'
(*Ib.* p. 363), are exposed to alteration and corruption,
and have consequently been altered and corrupted in
a far greater degree than mere ordinary words.
'No phonetic rules would suffice to help us to
discover the original form and meaning of such names
as London, York, or Birmingham' (*Ib.* p. 363).
Christian names 'have been tortured in different
languages to such a degree that no phonetic rules
would give us a key to their secret history'
(*Ib.* p. 365). To take an instance,—one which I am
sure will please Mr. Gomme,—of the change in a
local name:—

'It was very natural to discover in Wormingford,
the ford of the Wormings, *i.e.*, the sons of Worm,
and we all remember how the believers in universal
totemism discovered in these sons of Worm (*Archæo-
logical Review,* iii. 357) the descendants or the
worshippers of the worm or serpent, and therefore
the abstainers from worms and serpents as part of
their daily food. Phonetically there was nothing
to be said against this etymology. But the circumstances were against it' (*C.* 363). Withermondeford,
the Widemondeford of Domesday Book, had been

gradually changed (corrupted) into Wormingford. 'No one would build any phonetic rules on the successive changes which Withermondeford underwent before it became Wormingford, and yet no one would protest against their identification, though in defiance of all phonetic rules which govern the transition of old into modern English' (*Ib.* p. 364).

Exeunt Worm and his totem tribe.

VIII. Phonetic laws, so-called

What is Grimm's Law. 'Only a rule of observation' (*Ib.* p. 304). All so-called phonetic laws, like so-called 'laws of nature,' are, in truth, but a set of observations, liable at any moment to be controlled, reformed, or regulated by some fresh observation. To think otherwise is merely to make capital of our nescience. Yet these considerations in no way countenance linguistic laxity :—

'Phonetic laws, or, to use a more modest name, phonetic rules or observations, if once established, must, no doubt, be implicity obeyed; only we should always try to remember how large or how small the evidence is on which each single phonetic rule has been made to rest. We should also be careful not to reject at once any etymology if it offends against one or other of our many phonetic rules, particularly if it is otherwise quite satisfactory on material as well as on formal grounds' (*Ib.* p. 301).

But some 'phonetic pharisees' make us justly complain 'that historical, mythological, etymological, and philosophical questions are ordered to stand aside or ruled out of court whenever they conflict or seem to conflict with phonetic observations. The

idea that the phonetic rules of to-day could possibly
have to yield to the phonetic rules of to-morrow, or
to other arguments, is never entertained '(*Ib.* p. 300).

These considerations, and much more to the same
effect, with many cogent instances, are excellently
and most powerfully urged by Prof. Müller.

IX. Unexplained phonetic irregularities

To take two remarkable Greek instances of
phonetic irregularity at present inexplicable :—

' The Greek θεός, god, has been divorced from the
Sk. deva, bright and god, and deus in Latin,
simply on the ground of phonetic incompatibility.
But with all due respect for phonetic laws, my
respect for the logic of facts is too strong' to admit
belief in the propriety of this divorce. 'Why δ
should have become θ I honestly confess that I cannot
explain. . . . The Greek θεός, if not derived from
the root div, has found no other root as yet from
which it could have been derived, so as to account
for its meaning, as well as its form ' (*Ib.* p. 391).

Again :—

' Phonetic consciences might rebel against the
change in the name of Dêmêter of g into d, but so far
as the ancient Greeks are concerned there can be no
doubt that they had accepted Dêmêter as Gê-mêter
or Mother Earth. It is certainly strange that Gê,
so common in Greek, should in the name of the
goddess have been changed to Dê. . . . Strict
phoneticians would say that it was impossible. Still
as the irregularity occurs in a proper name it has
to be accepted, the material evidence being too strong

in favour of Dêmêter being an earth-goddess'
(*Ib.* p. 535).

I have always regarded the truth of the matter to
be as follows:—*When the names of two mythic
concepts, palpably identical in general character,
appear, although similar, to violate a phonetic rule,
such apparent violation, after making due allowance
for dialectic differences and changes in pronunciation
brought about by time, should be ascribed to the
operation of some other phonetic rule of which as yet
we are ignorant.* The same principle of course
applies to ordinary words. To know all is to understand all. Imperfect knowledge, even if great, has
its special dangers.

X. Solar Mythology

For a few years past some of the camp-followers
of the anthropological school have rejoiced to gird
and jeer at certain (non-existent) mythologists who
were supposed to endeavour 'to turn everything
into the sun.' This cackle is rapidly dying away.
The sun still holds the field as the protagonist in
mythology; and nearly all students now admit the
immense mass of solar myth, not specially Aryan,
but found universally dominant alike amongst Lets
and Fins, by the Nile and the Euphrates, in the New
World as in the Old, in fact, solarism everywhere.
If there be still anyone who doubts this, let him
take a good course of Hibbert Lectures; let him
read and mark Sir P. Renouf, *Religion of Ancient
Egypt* (1880), Prof. Sayce, *Religion of the Ancient
Babylonians* (1887), and Prof. Rhys, *Religion as
illustrated by Celtic Heathendom* (1888). Let him

then study the religions of Mexico and Peru. But, above all, let him listen to the voice of Mr. Lang :—

'Nobody has ever denied [Umps!] that gods who are the sun or live in the sun are familiar, and are the centres of myths among most races' (*M. M.* p. 133).

'It is a popular delusion that the anthropological mythologists deny the existence of solar myths, or of nature-myths in general' (*Ib.* p. 63).

You see, gentle reader, that harmony is now practically restored. Of course one occasionally meets with an eccentric view respecting this or that solar personage. Thus :—

'Mr. Frazer, Mannhardt's disciple, is very severe on solar theories of Osiris [Mercy on us! What will be heresy next?], and connects that god with the corn-spirit. But Mannhardt did not go so far, Mannhardt thought that the myth of Osiris was solar' (*Ib.* p. xxii).

Very sensible of him. The 'corn-spirit' is evidently mounting to Mr. Frazer's brain. If, following the example of Mr. Swiveller, I may adapt the words of a popular poet,—

O Mr. Frazer, Mr. Frazer, what a man you are !
I never thought when you set out that you would "go so far." '

Again :—

'Mannhardt takes the [famous and now familiar] old Egyptian tale of "The Two Brothers"' (*Ib.* p. 59), and declares, 'The *Märchen* is an old obscure solar myth' (*Ib.* p. 61).

But :—

'Mr. Frazer, Mannhardt's disciple [and 'prophet,'

Ib. p. 43], protests *à grand cris* against these identifications when made by others than Mannhardt' (*Ib.* p. 61).

Not quite consistent of Mr. Frazer. And here it is necessary for Mr. Lang to warn us that :—

'A tendency to seek for exclusively vegetable origins of gods is to be observed in some of the most recent speculations' (*Ib.* p. xxiii).

This may be called the Covent-garden-market theory of mythology, and is evidently dangerously seductive. Well may Mr. Lang style *The Golden Bough*, 'that entrancing book' (*Ib.* p. 42).

XI. Light thrown by the Veda on Greek Mythology

Many admirable instances are given by Prof. Müller of how Vedic words, names, expressions, modes of thought, and legends light up the obscure places of Greek mythology. To take an instance. We read in Homer :—

' Fair-tressed Demeter yielded to her love, and lay with Iasion in the thrice-ploughed fallow field' (*Od.* v. 125-7. Ap. Butcher and Lang).

This is a dark saying. We know indeed that Dêmêtêr is the Earth, orderly and cultivated ; and that her fair tresses = her golden grain. But we must go to the *Veda* to see that Iasiôn (Vide *sup.* p. 7) = Vivasvân, *i.e.*, the Sun. Then we understand Dêmêtêr's love affair, no modern novel-story of unbridled passion, but the influence of the Sun upon the Earth, making her fruitful; whilst Triptolemos, Dêmêtêr's henchman, a hero of civiliz-ation and fabled inventor of the plough, is simply the Thrice-ploughed-field ($\tau\rho i\pi o\lambda o\varsigma$) personified.

Observe how perfectly the material features of the myth harmonize with the true linguistic interpretation of the names of the personages concerned ; and how clear a light each side casts upon the other. We look in vain *e.g.*, to totemism for any such illumination of human thought. We only find the melancholy admission that totemism is itself inexplicable. Says Mr. Lang :—

‘ The origin of totemism is unknown to me, as to McLennen and Robertson Smith ’ (*M. M.* p. 75).

It is unnecessary here to add further instances of Prof. Müller’s use of the *Veda* in illustration of Greek mythology. The Dêmêtêr-Iasiôn myth is at once a perfect example of his system and of its success.

XII. Novel Etymologies

Novel etymologies will of course crop up from time to time. Whether this circumstance is a reason for discarding linguistics, I shall consider later. To take one or two. Mannhardt, ‘ for the man was mortal,’ quotes Mr. Lang, gave an extraordinary ‘ guess ’ at Dêmêtêr. He thought it $= \zeta\epsilon\iota\grave{\alpha}\ \delta\eta + \mu\acute{\eta}\tau\eta\rho =$ ‘ Corn-mother’ (Vide *M. M.* p. 54). Has he on this point one ‘ disciple ’ in the world? Prof. Bechtel has recently amused us with some wondrous etymological conjectures. Thus Dionysos, he thinks is derived from *Dios* and *snutya* which latter word we find might mean ‘ fed on mother milk ’ (*C.* p. 373). He takes Dionysos ‘ as originally a form of Zeus ’; but, as Prof. Müller observes, the identity [of Dionysos] with his father . . . is a strong demand on our faith, or rather on our credulity ’ (*Ib.*). Moreover, as Prof. Müller shows, Prof. Bechtel, in this instance,

flings 'the phonetic rules' overboard. He next
attacks Aphrodîtê, poor creature, and we learn with
astonishment 'that the first name given to this
goddess of love was connected with fordus, pregnant,
and because she encouraged love and marriage [Did
she encourage marriage?] she is supposed [by Prof.
Bechtel] to have been celebrated as the Pregnant
Woman' (*Ib.* p. 386). Indeed. *Distinguo.* Love is
one thing, marriage another, and pregnancy a third.
They are by no means necessarily connected with
each other. 'Fortunately,' continues Prof. Müller,
'the very author of this etymology is afraid of the
consequences which it would involve.' Well he
may be. Aphrodîtê is certainly connected with
marriage, but merely as a Love-goddess. Let us
pass from such phantasies to a really scientific
conjecture. We are well aware what a crux the
name Apollôn has been. Semitic derivations have
been suggested, but they are impossible because
Apollôn is a thoroughly Aryan god. 'The ancients
derived 'Aπόλλων from 'απόλλ-υμι in the sense of
destroyer. . . Phonetically there is nothing to be
said against it. . But we cannot decide on an
etymology by means of phonetic laws only. The
meaning also has a right to be considered. Now we
have no right to say that from the beginning
Apollon was a destructive god' (*C.* p. 689), an
Apollyôn. And then Prof. Müller, with very great
learning and ability, proceeds to show that Apollôn
would correspond with such a Sk. form as *Apa-var-
yan or *Apa-val-yan, and that such a form would
mean 'the Opener,' *i.e.*, of the heavenly gates, eastern
and western, with which the sun and also Apollôn
are so much connected. 'Phonetically there is no

2

possible objection ' (*Ib.* p. 694) to this derivation, which also exactly corresponds with the original central thought of the concept of Apollôn, as a Sun-god. But admirable as this suggestion is, Prof. Müller by no means lays it down as a dogma. He is, however, fully entitled to the opinion that it is by far the best explanation yet offered; and that therefore, at all events for the present and until a better explanation is forthcoming, it justly holds the field. He well adds, ' In matters like these . . we ought not to clamour for mathematical certainty ' (*Ib.* p. 695).

XIII. 'The Lesson of Jupiter'

According to the very severe Prof. Macdonell (*Vedic Mythology*, p. 8), the equation, ' Dyaus = Ζεύς is . . beyond the range of doubt' (Vide *M. M.* p. 201 ; *sup.* p. 9). Here, then, we stand on *terra-firma*. But what does this admission involve ? On this question Prof. Müller remarks :—

' Those who are fond of scoffing at the labours of such men as Kuhn, Bréal, Darmesteter and others, fall down before Zeus = Jupiter = Dyaus. They believe in the father of the devas, but not in his sons and daughters ' (*C.* p. 529).

' That the Aryan mythologies spring from a common source, the one equation of Dyaush-pitar, Ζεὺς πατήρ, and Ju-piter has placed once for all beyond the reach of all reasonable doubt ' (*Ib.* p. 451).

' Even the most stubborn opponents of all attempts at tracing Greek and Indian gods back to a common source seem to have yielded an unwilling assent to the relationship between the Greek Ζεὺς πατήρ, the

Vedic Dyaush-pitar, the Latin Jupiter, and the Teutonic Týr. But they do not seem to have perceived that in making this concession they have in reality conceded everything, or at all events the fundamental principle of scientific mythology. If it is once admitted that the Supreme God of the ancient [Aryan] world was known under one and the same name before the ancestors of Hindus, Greeks, Romans, and Germans became permanently separated, and that the name of that Deity has survived in the most ancient literary relics of every one of these nations, it would surely seem to follow that this could not have been the only name which thus survived. If the word for ten is the same in the principal Aryan languages, should we not be surprised to find that all the other numerals were different?' (*Ib.* p. 498).

To this pellucid presentation of the argument it is surely needless to make any addition. Nothing much short of a miracle could prevent the existence of other 'equations.' But the foregoing considerations point also to another important truth. S. Paul, ever a 'sound divine,' makes the further equation— Zeus = God (*Acts*, xvii. 28). The Zeus of the noble poems of Aratos and Kleanthês is God Himself, and no meaner Being. And even if philological comparative mythology had taught us nothing else, we should still most justly revere her for this, that she has demonstrated in a manner 'that cannot be spoken against,' that our common ancestors, however ignorant and erring they may have been, yet worshipped, after their fashion, no less a Being than the almighty and everlasting God.

2 *

Such, then, is Prof. Müller's final standpoint, mythological and linguistic. Throughout his book he supports his position with all that wealth of illustration and fulness of knowledge which are so peculiarly his own. Into further philological detail it is needless for me to enter, especially since Mr. Lang cares nought for such matters ; and I quite agree with the Professor's general linguistic method in its application to Aryan words and names. Mr. Lang, as I understand him, regards the study of linguistics in connexion with mythology as absolutely worthless. To him Prof. Müller's philology is neither better nor worse than that of Prof. Bechtel, or of Mr. Casaubon. The whole thing is vanity.

XIV. Where I disagree with Prof. Müller

My objection to Prof. Müller's position is, briefly, that he almost absolutely ignores the vast force and extent of Semitic influence in Hellas, *i.e.*, Continental Greece and her colonies; and passes over, with the slightest and most inadequate notice, the writers who have demonstrated this important fact. Because the Greeks were an Aryan nation, because Zeus, Aïdôneus, Hêra, Dêmêtêr, Apollôn, Athêna, Arês, Hêphaistos, Hermês, Hestia, Pan (= Πάων, ' the Herdsman.' Roscher.), etc., were Aryan divinities, whose names, concepts, and histories are rightly to be interpreted on Aryan lines ; therefore, he practically assumes, the whole Pantheon is Aryan. I do not accept this conclusion. I say that the evidence, the logic of facts historical and linguistic, is against this part of his theory. The Aryan principle, the philology, the history which so well explains Zeus and his real (not merely artificial) family, fails when applied to

Kronos, Poseidôn, Dionysos, Aphrodîtê, and many other personages of Hellenic mythology. This view of the matter, I shall endeavour to support in the Third Part of the present work. Thus, whilst the reader will perceive that I am no mere blind devotee of Prof. Müller, the latter, should he ever read these pages, will do me the justice to believe that I understand and appreciate his system; and will accept my assurance that I yield to none in admiration for his profound learning and splendid achievements. Fifty years of strenuous and sagacious effort have placed upon his brow a crown which the whirligig of time will be powerless to remove, let Carp and Pike try their best, or their worst.

PART II

MR. LANG'S LATEST ATTACK UPON PROFESSOR MÜLLER

I. Mr. Andrew Lang

AT the present time there are few British litera-
teurs more widely known than Mr. Andrew Lang.
The field of his activity is so large and his energy
is so untiring, that he is almost always in evidence.
He appeals to all sorts and conditions of men.
Have we a taste for the Classics? He can translate
Homer, and descant upon the Epic with equal
facility. Have we a leaning towards literature
generally, he can hold forth on books and bookmen,
and write to Dead Authors. Do we like verse? He
can produce it to any extent and of excellent
quality. Have we a weakness for a novel? He
supplies one with the utmost ease. He is equally at
home with Dreams, or the Cock Lane Ghost, or the
'Awful Apparition that appeared to Lord Lyttleton.'
Do we want a good heavy book (and some people
do)? He is ready for us with over 700 pages on
myths, ritual, and religion. He is the founder, or,
at all events, the most well known figure, of a
peculiar school of anthropological mythology.
Classical performer (he objects to the term
'scholar'), translator, editor, novelist, poet, ghost-
story collector, anthropologist, and I know not what
besides, he is indeed a many-sided man. But when
we add to all this the fact that he is a professional
critic and reviewer, that his journalistic activity is

very great, that he is an habitual contributor to many
prominent magazines, a friend of any number of
literary men, and withal a past-master in the art
of flouts, jibes and jeers ; it will be seen that
Hêraklês himself, had he tackled such an opponent
with either club or pen, might probably have
deemed that he had all his work cut out for him.
And I am here the more reminded of the Son of
Alkmênê, on account of the journalistic position
of Mr. Lang, who can smite you with the spear
of totemistic anthropology in the columns of the
Daily News, scalp and tomahawk you generally
in the *Saturday Review*, and transfix you with the
fine arrows of his sarcasm monthly in *Longman's
Magazine*. He is thus a species of literary Geryôn,
a *Tricorpor*, a kind of (if, for the moment, he will
pardon the equation) Sârvara-Kerberos, ' three
gentlemen at once.'

II. Mr. Lang and Prof. Max Müller

Naaman had much to be thankful for, and Ahab
was doubtless a fairly rich man; but yet we all
want something. And so it chanced that Mr. Lang,
despite the position which his brilliant abilities
and tireless industry had won for him, had a secret
cause of dissatisfaction and discontent. It fell out
thus. He had often 'reviewed' (a pleasant
expression frequently signifying ' to hold up to
scorn and contempt') Prof. Müller; and, to his own
satisfaction and to that of certain of his friends,
had shown the worthlessness of the Professor's
linguistic and mythological opinions. He had even
expended no small store of jibes and jeers on the
Professor and ' the inevitable Dawn,' which will

persist (thank God) in reappearing every morning. But although he had done all this and more; and had, in addition, excogitated a totem-bear and a totem-mouse, wound them up and set them a-working,—machinery in motion,—in regions Hellenic; yet still, strange and sad to say, the tranquil sage continued to labour on quietly, and did not even so much as mention Mr. Lang in any of his books (Vide *C.* p. 184). Such a situation was intolerable; but, although the days of the duello have unfortunately gone by, there was still a way out of it. I gather that a kind of deputation waited upon Prof. Müller to point out to him his incivility in the matter; and to urge him to amend his manners by at once making an attack in writing on Mr. Lang. The Professor himself states :—

'I have been told, both in public and in private, that it was hardly civil to leave the criticisms of such men as Mr. Herbert Spencer and Mr. Andrew Lang unnoticed and unanswered' (*C.* p. 3).

The courteous veteran pleads in extenuation, that he thought 'personal controversy' did more harm than good; that many of the opinions now again advanced he had replied to long ago; and that as for 'their latest or loudest advocates,' he 'felt considerable difficulty how to deal with some of their criticisms or rather witticisms, without seeming either harsh or discourteous.' In the true spirit of the gentleman, he adds :—

'I have always admired Mr. Herbert Spencer as a hard worker and as a hard thinker, I admire Mr. Andrew Lang as a charming poet and brilliant writer.'

It is almost touching to see the old man thus dragged into the fray; however, he intended to write the *Contributions*, as a summary of his case and position, and in this work he has obligingly made some references to Mr. Lang's theories and opinions.

This, though a point gained, did not altogether satisfy Mr. Lang, who evidently wanted a line by line sort of Mill-upon-Hamilton examination of his works by Prof. Müller. However, his 'adversary' (*M. M.* p. 200. 'For adversary we must consider Mr. Max Müller.' It quite reminds us of the evil god ' Chaitan—obviously Shaitan,' *Ib.* p. 132) had at length written another book ; and, what was wanted, put Mr. Lang's name in it. So the industrious man promptly sat down and reeled off *Modern Mythology*, in which in the space of less than 200 pages (for a portion of the work is ' constructive,' and does not refer to Prof. Müller) he purports again to pulverize the latter, and to show up all his weakness, especially his ' disease of language.'

III. Mr. Lang's View of Philology

As Mrs. Squeers was no grammarian, so Mr. Lang, doubtless with equal thankfulness, is no philologist :—

' Etymologies, of course, I leave to be discussed by scholars ' (*Ib.* p. 137).

He may well let them alone, for he asserts, evidently with (for the moment) honest conviction :—

' There is no name named among men which a philologist cannot easily prove to be a synonym or metaphorical term for wind or weather, dawn or sun (*Ib.* p. 135).

But although regardless of philology, he is death on logic. *Caesarem appellasti; ad Caesarem ibis.* Mr. Lang must (I may presume) have carefully read Prof. Müller's *Contributions.* He will therefore know that the Professor is unable to explain such familiar names as Olympos, Aphroditê, and Artemis. He does know this, for he says :—

' As to the meaning and derivation of Artemis, our Author [*i.e.*, Prof. Müller] knows   nothing ' (*Ib.* p. 147).

But ' our Author ' is a very great philologist.

Argal : the proposition, *There is no name named among men which a philologist cannot easily prove to be a synonym or metaphorical term for wind or weather, dawn or sun,* IS FALSE.

' What trick, what device, what starting hole, canst thou now find out, to hide thee ? '

Perhaps ' our Author ' may reply that he *didn't mean what he said.* This may be so, but such an admission at once makes his whole work worthless. But that we may be well satisfied he did mean what he said, hear him again :—

' We only oppose the philological attempt to *account for all the features in a god's myth* [Italics mine.] as manifestations of the elemental qualities denoted by *a name which may mean at pleasure* [Italics mine.] dawn, storm, clear air, thunder, wind. twilight, water, *or what you will* ' (*Ib.* p. 133, Italics mine).

Thus, to Mr. Lang, philology, with respect to

the names of gods, is simply 'a gallimaufrey of gambols,' a kind of 'Twelfth Night or What you Will.' But is this so? Take the familiar name of Hêraklês. What 'pleasure' Prof. Müller would feel if he could explain it. According to Mr. Lang, the Professor could make it mean ' dawn, etc.,' just as he liked. As a matter of fact Prof. Müller can't explain the hero's name (Vide *C.* pp. 612, 632). Therefore this representation of the matter by Mr. Lang is as incorrect as his previous proposition above noticed.

Mr. Lang's (real or assumed) ignorance of philology saves him from the trouble of noticing about five-sixths of Prof. Müller's work, which, nevertheless, he yet ventures to condemn as practically worthless and misleading. From what he says, I gather that if anyone asked him such a question as, ' But you will surely admit that Dyaus = Zeus?' he would reply, ' Well, really, I can't pretend to say. I leave such matters to " scholars " and other triflers.'

The unreasonableness of this attitude may be seen by a parallel case. Suppose you are talking about history with someone, and, apropos of what was being said, you remark, 'I presume you don't doubt that Richard I. was King of England?' What would be thought of the man who replied, 'Well, really I don't concern myself with such matters. It may be as you suggest; but my name is not Gardiner, and certainly it is not—Green.'

Thus might we leave history to historians, law to lawyers, divinity to divines, and so on, perhaps contenting ourselves with some such humble indulgence as, *e.g.*, a mouse-totem.

IV. 'No gentleman ever consciously misrepresents'

'No gentleman or honest man,' says Mr. Lang, 'ever *consciously* misrepresents the ideas of an opponent. . . It is always *unconsciously* that adversaries [who are gentlemen] pervert, garble, and misrepresent' (*M. M.* 92-3).

I agree; but I regret to say that a 'gentleman' is often guilty of what may be called most reprehensible negligence in his representations. Observe Mr. Lang's statement above quoted :—

'We only oppose *the philological attempt to account for all the features in a god's myth as manifestations of the elemental qualities denoted by* ' the god's name.

Mr. Lang would be quite right to oppose such an attempt, but nobody makes it.

He says :—

'That Zeus means " sky " cannot conceivably explain scores of details in the very composite legend of Zeus—say, the story of Zeus, Demeter, and the Ram' (*Ib.* p. xviii).

Referring to the admirable work of my friend Mr. D. G. Hogarth, *Philip and Alexander of Macedon,* he remarks :—

'As Mr. Hogarth points out, Alexander has inherited in the remote East the myths of early legendary heroes. We cannot explain these by the analysis of the name of Alexander' (*Ibid.*).

To this I reply, ' Who deniges of it, Mr. Lang ? ' And, to give my question ' a deeper and more awful character of solemnity,' I repeat it, ' Mr. Lang, who deniges of it ? ' When and where has Prof. Müller, or anyone else, said that the name 'Zeus' will explain all the details related about Zeus ? What he does say is that ' etymology is an immense help,' but that ' Comparative Mythology could exist and light up more or less the darkest corners of mythology in every part of the world . . . if not a single name of any god or hero had been preserved or could be analysed etymologically ' (*C.* p. 781). He does not pretend to explain all that has been stated about Zeus, either by means of philology or of anything else. Thus he says : —

' To explain all the love affairs of Zeus would be difficult, *if not impossible* (*C.* p. 518. Italics mine).

Now I ask Mr. Lang, How comes he to misrepresent Professor Müller so gravely ? And the only answer I can suggest is, that Mr. Lang is in such a hurry to polish off his opponent, and to get on to something more important, such as *Dreams and Ghosts*, that he cannot take the trouble to grasp Professor Müller's real position. Thus he here merely sets up a man of straw which anyone could knock down, and thereby (practically) tries to throw dust into the eyes of the reader.

Thus, too, when some years ago I published a work on a portion of the *Odyssey*, hardly had it appeared, when it was attacked with the utmost contempt and derision in the *Saturday Review* by a ' critic' whose style and standpoint were exactly those of Mr. Lang. I made no objection to the contempt and derision ; but there was another feature in this attack to which I did take exception. The Editor of the *Academy* was, very properly, fond of a fair field and no favour ; and he opened his columns to a discussion upon some

of the points in question, in which controversy,
between some of my literary friends and myself on
the one hand and Mr. Lang on the other, according
to general opinion the brilliant journalist came off
but second best. I said :—

'It is refreshing to turn from the misrepresenta-
tions of the *Saturday Review* critic who recently
attacked my *Myth of Kirkê*, to the cautious language
of Mr. A. Lang in the *Academy*. My critic, after
saying, " Mr. Brown's arguments are *something like*
this "—just as a caricature is something like the
original—thus distorts my view : " Odysseus lived
in a cave, therefore Odysseus is the sun ; " and then
makes a reference to Robinson Crusoe in order "to
set on some quantity of barren spectators to laugh."
I can only rejoin that I never said anything of the
kind.'

And, when noticing Mr. Lang's objection to the
mythological method of Sir Geo. Cox, I say that here
again,

'The same unfortunate misrepresentation of the
matter occurs. Mr. Lang says, " That method rests
on the philological interpretation of the names," and
is " the exclusively philological method." But Sir
George says, " Assuredly neither Odysseus, Herakles,
nor any other can be the sun, unless their names, *their
general character, and their special features* carry us
to this conclusion."'

Thus, alike in the cases of Prof. Müller and Sir
Geo. Cox, we find Mr. Lang most seriously mis-
representing his opponents. Well may he protest
that the 'gentleman' only errs in this way by

accident. Well, then, let the 'gentleman' be more careful for the future.

V. The 'gentleman' never unfair

As the 'gentleman' never wilfully misrepresents, so, doubtless, he is never unfair. Yet at times it is hard to realize this.

I have always regarded the *Encyclopædia Britannica* as being singularly unfortunate in its treatment of mythology (Vide *inf.* p. 212). In the last edition Mr. Lang, after giving his views on this subject, refers to my *Great Dionysiak Myth,* and observes that it contains 'many useful references,' but that 'the reasonings need not be adopted.' In a sense this is, of course, a truism; but was it really necessary, in such a very general treatment of the subject, and in a work like the *Encyclopædia Britannica,* to name a particular book merely because it contained 'useful references?' Was it quite needful to warn the babes and sucklings who were likely to read this Article, against being led away by my (supposed) subtle errors? Or rather did not Mr. Lang, just after a controversy with me, gladly take the opportunity to stereotype his dislike of my opinions (which, at the same time, he made no attempt to refute) by a wholly unnecessary reference to them, treating them with the utmost contempt, in a great work which most people would trustfully accept as a standard authority? Says Mr. Lang, in *The New Review :*—

'The writings of critics are often so ignorant, so prejudiced, so spiteful, so careless, that perhaps no

printed matter is more entirely valueless, and contemptible.'

This testimony is doubtless true.

VI. Mr. Lang on 'competing etymologies'

But the reader may naturally ask, How can
Mr. Lang, if ignorant of philology, venture to sit in
judgment on and to condemn a work by the most
prominent philologist of the day, and five-sixths of
which is occupied with philological considerations ?
Mr. Lang's answer is, that, although he professes to
know nothing anent philological Comparative Mythology, its votaries have given it away by their
differences of opinion ; and that we may therefore
unhesitatingly reject it. This position I will, therefore, next examine. Apart from philology however,
Mr. Lang informs us that he possesses a 'smattering
of unscholarly learning' (*M. M.* p. 200) ; and is
doubtless, therefore, well equipped for the fray. Says
Mr. Lang :—

'Nothing irritates philological mythologists so
much, nothing has injured them so much in the
esteem of the public which " goes into these things a
little," as the statement that their competing etymologies and discrepent interpretations of mythical
names are mutually destructive. I have been told
that this is " a mean argument "' (*M. M.* p. 50).

If this or any other argument be sound, it need not
fear being called 'mean.'   But, first notice the gallery
to which Mr. Lang specially plays. It is composed
of Those - who - go - into - these - things - a - little. These
persons, thus confessedly knowing but little, are
naturally well competent to judge of much. In fact

3

they know just enough to be somewhat amused and confused by Mr. Lang's pleasantries. Odysseus was the sun, therefore Robinson Crusoe was the sun. What an excellent jest, and how those readers of the *Saturday*, 'who go into these things a little,' must have roared at it ! It is the people that go into matters a little, who hold that the English nation are the Ten Tribes, and a thousand other phantasies, from which the man who can't go into them at all is fortunately preserved.

Let us next examine that cardinal dogma of Mr. Lang's on which his condemnation of Prof. Müller's position mainly rests. We learn that :—

' Competing etymologies and discrepent interpretations are mutually destructive.' These differences are, of course, differences of opinion ; therefore differences of opinion (it seems) are mutually destructive. Let us test this further, for Mr. Lang is nothing if not logical. I think of the number 9, and ask A, B, and C to guess what number I have thought of. A guesses 3, B 6, C 9. Are these differences of opinion 'mutually destructive ?' Surely C is right, and the other two wrong. So if Athêna is said to be the Moon (Porphyry), the Lightning (Roscher), or the Dawn (Müller), why are these views 'mutually destructive.' Why may not one of them be correct ? In the abstract Athêna may= Anything, and Mr. Lang, of all men, has no right to say that any of these views are wrong ; since, admittedly, he has no knowledge on the matter. But, it may be urged, in so doubtful a case, is it safe to come to any positive conclusion ? Well, to suspend judgment is in many mythological cases

absolutely necessary ; and Mr. Lang, once thought so
(Vide *Myth, Ritual, and Religion*, ii. 250). But now
he promptly condemns the whole lot as 'mutually
destructive.' And observe, in passing, there is a
general and absolute consensus amongst these sages
that Athêna represents some natural phenomenon.
They are all disciples of the Natural Phenomena
Theory. So are Welcker, Preller, Schwartz, Lauer,
Furtwängler, and nearly everyone else who has
closely studied the Athêna-myth.

VII.   Another 'Competing Etymology' fallacy

Another fallacy which underlies Mr. Lang's treatment of competing etymologies is that they are all of
equal value. The mathematical odds are x to 1
against this. Several writers lately have apparently
held that if Mr. A. B. differs from Prof. Müller on
any point, the latter must necessarily be wrong.
Thus, because many years ago Benfey connected
'Athêna' with the Zend *athayana*, a conjecture which
was long ago refuted, we are given to understand
that this etymon is quite as good as any other and
later ones. Curtius again made a *conjecture*, nothing
more, respecting the derivation of the name.
Speaking of the root ἀθ, he says, 'whence *perhaps*
comes Athene.' Preller preferred to connect 'Athêna'
with αἰθ, 'whence αἴθηρ, "the air," or ἀνθ, whence
ἄνθος, "a flower."' He evidently *knew* nothing on
the matter, and, as Mr. Lang observes, ' He does not
regard these etymologies as certain.' Very wise of
him. These suggestions of Benfey, Curtius, and
Preller are tentative and conjectural, *mere* suggestions,
as their authors would freely admit. And it is further

3 *

assumed that they would still hold to them in the face
of much more evidence to the contrary, a point which
is by no means certain. Prof. Bechtel again explains,

'Athêne very simply, no doubt, by Athanatos, the
immortal, but how Athanatos was shortened to
Athêne, and why Athêne alone was called Athanatos,
the immortal, we are not told ' (*C*. p. 378).

As against such suggestions as these, which at best
would be what the lawyers call ' bare possibilities,'
Prof. Müller equates Athêna with the Vedic Ahanâ
(' the Dawn'), proves to the hilt that this equation is
' phonetically irreproachable,' and further that the
central features of the Athêna-concept are also in
agreement with the idea of a Dawn-goddess. Here is
a view which although of course not a mathematical
certainty fairly holds· the field. None of the other
scholars who have treated of the Athêna-myth have
been able to equate the goddess with a corresponding
Aryan analogue. According to Furtwängler, the
voice of Athêna is the thunder, but he can point to
no analogous Aryan Thunder-goddess; and the voice
of Athêna will equally well represent the thousand
voices and sounds of the morning. Yes, Mr. Lang
may say, and it may equally well represent a dozen
other things. Not so. At this point in the enquiry
the sword of philological Comparative Mythology is
thrown into the balance, which therefore inclines in
favour of the view of Prof. Müller. I have noticed
divers sneers at his philology. This or that
instance, we are told, was good enough for the fifties
or sixties, and so on. But the Athêna-Ahanâ equation has been carefully tested and re-tested by
Prof. Müller (Vide *C*. pp. 406-8), and is quite up to

date. Sneers cannot affect the question, and he is perfectly justified in saying :—

' That Athêne or Athăna was originally a representative of the light of the morning, then of light and wisdom in general, born from the head of Dyaus (Divo mûrdhna*h*), and that her name is the same as the Vedic Ahanâ, is as certain as anything can be in comparative mythology' (*C.* p. 378).

VIII. Reasonable effect of differences of opinion

Says Mr. Lang :—

' In all sciences there are differences of opinion about details ' (*M. M.* p. 2). He does not hold that we should regard them as worthless on this account; but proceeds to say that :—

' In comparative mythology there was, with rare exceptions, no agreement at all about results; except indeed that everybody agreed that Aryan myths were in the immense majority of instances, to be regarded as mirror-pictures on earth, of celestial and meteorological phenomena' (*Ibid.*).

But surely this was an astonishing agreement on a general principle; and it would be easy to show by hundreds of instances, that there was likewise a very considerable agreement in matters of detail, necessitating a further agreement respecting results. Mr. Lang would be wholly unable to prove his assertion, and naturally does not attempt to do so.

The points of disagreement among votaries of the Natural Phenomena Theory chiefly occur in connexion with the names, and, to some extent, with the concepts of a few prominent divinities, *e.g.*, Athêna.

These cases being familiar, make the want of agreement appear to be far more extensive than it really
is.   And what are they, when they loom largest, but
' differences of opinion about details,' and therefore,
according to Mr. Lang, should not prove fatal
to the science.   I shall show also that frequently,
e.g., in the case of Hêrmes, these differences are far
more apparent than real.

But supposing that in a science or belief there are
differences, not merely about details, but also about
principles of very grave importance, do we therefore
at once reject it ?   Take the instance of Religion,
or narrow it to Christianity.   Is this at once to go
overboard because men differ on the question of the
Double Procession, Episcopacy, or the Sacraments?
Surely such matters as these are hardly mere details ;
but, if Christianity is therefore worthless as a belief,
scheme, or science, on account of such differences, let
us be told so.

Astronomy, Political Economy (including currency
questions), Geology, have all exhibited by their
votaries the widest difference in principles, and not
merely in details; but who would therefore abandon
any one of them as worthless or delusive?

IX.   Differences of opinion apparent rather than real

Many differences of opinion amongst mythologists
are apparent rather than real.   Take the case of
Hermês.   According to Dr.   Roscher (*Hermes der
Windgott*) and Sir Geo. Cox, he represents the Wind.
Mr. Ruskin, in his beautiful *Queen of the Air* (i. 29),
which, like his other works, combines such
marvellous insight and exquisite expression, coupled

often with most dubious statements, calls Hermês
'the Lord of Cloud.' All quite true, yet not the
whole truth. Many of the Greek gods, like most of
the Vedic gods, are far more complex in character
than this, and Hermês is one of these. Says Prof.
Müller:—

'Menand takes him for the twilight, so does Ploix,
and Mehlis sees in him a general solar deity. Instead
of trying to understand why these scholars differ from
each other, their divergence has been represented as
the surest proof of their incompetence. Still Darwin
and Agassiz were allowed to differ without being
called hard names, nor was Comparative Physiology
tabooed because it was progressive.

'The divergence between these scholars was
chiefly due to their attempting to circumscribe too
narrowly the activity of the ancient gods. Hermês, as
the son of Saramâ, belongs certainly to the dawn and
the twilight, but the morning wind belongs by right
to the same domain, and as the twilight of morning
and evening was frequently conceived as one [Like the
'star of the morn and eve.'], the god of the morning
may and will finish his course as god of the evening.
In this way the various characters of Hermes, as
messenger of the gods, as winged, as the robber of the
cows, and as musician, may all be traced back to one
and the same original concept.

'Nor does the view of Mehlis (*Die Grundidee des
Hermes*, 1877) interfere at all with the other explanations of Hermes, for Hermes as the son of the dawn
may well be called a solar deity, only not a solar
deity in general, but one of many agents discovered in the morning sun. If we take this more

comprehensive and at the same time more natural
view of Hermes, we shall see how nearly all his
epithets harmonize with his original character'
(*C*. p. 678).

There is very little of real contradiction in all this;
only a certain imperfection of treatment by persons
harmoniously using the same general principle. As
if a life of Richard I. merely treated of him as King
of England, ignoring the fact that he was also Duke
of Normandy. As regards epithets, the general concept of a divinity is best arrived at by a thorough
analysis of all his ancient epithets which are not
merely place-names, including of course his principal
name or protagonistic epithet.

X. Differences amongst Anthropologists

Anthropological mythologists differ amongst themselves even as others; but how absurd it would be to
pour ridicule and contempt upon their researches as
a whole, because, forsooth, where Mannhardt sees a
sun-god, Mr. Lang may find a totem, whilst Mr.
Frazer may behold a corn-spirit. Mr. Lang (very
properly) notes such instances of difference; and it is
impossible but that these causes of offence must come.
But heaven forbid that I should deride the valuable
researches of able men on any such ground as this.
All intelligent errors are useful. They set us thinking carefully; they frequently indicate where truth
lies, and often powerfully assist us in demonstrating
its force. And this fact I will next try to illustrate
by a consideration of the myth of Dêmêtêr-Erinnys,
as Pausanias spells the name.

XI. The Myth of Dêmêtêr-Erinnys

There are some instances of mythic interpretation where everyone has hitherto gone wrong ; neither A, B, nor C has guessed the Hyponoia. And, when this is the case, the underlying reason of such failure often consists in the fact, that a method, excellent in itself, has been incorrectly pressed into the service. As the Arkadian legend of Dêmêtêr-Erinnys has of late been much handled by various writers, including Prof. Müller and Mr. Lang, I shall deal with the facts as briefly as possible.

Near Thelpousa at a place called Onkeion reigned Onkos, according to tradition a son of Apollôn. Here it was (and none of those who have handled the myth have paid any attention to this circumstance) that Poseidôn (Mr. Farnell, *Cults of the Greek States*, i. 3, note, by a slip reads ' Kronos ') followed Dêmêtêr. She changed herself into a mare to avoid him, but he changed himself into a horse ; and she became by him the mother of Despoina ('the Mistress ') and the horse Areiôn (' Better ', *i.e.*, than other horses). She was enraged at the outrage, and got the name Erinnys from her anger, because the Arkadians call being angry ἐρινύειν. The same story, with a variant detail, was also told at Phigaleia, near which place was an ancient statue of Black Dêmêtêr. The goddess was represented in human form, except that she had a mare's head and mane, with figures of serpents and wild beasts about her head. In one hand she held a dolphin, in the other a dove. Pausanias sagely adds, ' They call the goddess Black because she has a black garment ' (Vide Paus. VIII. xxv, xlii). Such, briefly, is the story.

Prof. Müller endeavours to explain the tale by
another from the *Veda*, a course which *primâ facie*
is quite unexceptionable. This latter story, now
familiar to students, tells how the world came
together at the wedding of Tvasht*ri*'s daughter;
how the mother of Yama, the wife of the great
Vivasvat, vanished; how they gave one like her to
Vivasvat; 'when that had taken place she bore the
two A*s*vins, and Sara*n*yû left behind the two twin
couples' (Vide *C.* p. 539). Here the Rishi, like
Homer, refers briefly to a famous story with which
his hearers were well acquainted. The great Vedic
commentator Yâska, who lived at least as early as
B.C. 500, explains the allusions just as Eustathios
and Servius interpret passages in Homer and Vergil.
Sara*n*yû, we learn, ' assumed the form of a mare and
ran away. Vivasvat, assuming likewise an equine
form, came together with her, and hence the two
A*s*vins were born'. Mr. Farnell·suggests, very
groundlessly, that, as the Hymn does not expressly
say that Sara*n*yû took the form of a mare, therefore
this incident 'may be a mere aetiological invention
of the commentator' (*Cults*, i. 2-3, note). Truly it
may, but the probabilities are infinitely against such
a theory. The poet does not give more detail because
he is merely noticing a familiar tale *en passant*. How
absurd it would be to suppose that when Eustathios
or Servius add similar detailed information, they are
' inventing!' What proof is there that such was the
character of Yâska, or of ancient Indian commenta-
tors generally? The whole circumstances leave no
reasonable doubt that the mare-myth was familiar to
the Vedic poet. Mr. Lang thinks so; and goes so
far as to say that these two stories make him incline

to or perhaps actually accept the hypothesis 'that the ancestors of Greek and Vedic peoples once dwelt together, had a common stock of savage fables, and a common or kindred language' (Vide *sup.* p. 5).

Now, what do these two stories when compared with each other really show? This, and no more: that nothing is more natural than for archaic man to imagine his gods as assuming animal forms. Why should he think thus? Well, take the Vedic tale. The sun suggests the Sun-god; the Sun-god speeds across heaven, he races, he is a racer, he is a horse (*i.e.,* 'Runner,' 'Racer,' Sk. *asva*, Zend *aspa*, Slav. *aszvà*, Gk. ἵππος, ἵκκος, Lat. *equus*, Teut. *ëhu*). A horse follows a mare; the sun catches up the dawn, the dawn comes to be spoken of as a mare. From a horse and a mare come offspring, so comes it from sun and dawn. The element of twins shows no necessary connexion in origin of the two stories. Such an idea might arise independently all over the world. Men were confronted with a great duality in many variant phases, light and darkness, day and night, sun and moon, dawn and even, morning and evening star, etc. The Vedic tale is admittedly concerned with celestial phenomena, and its archaic simplicity of thought enables us to comprehend that the animal-transformation in the obscurer story may be a very natural mode of thought. This way of regarding natural phenomena is said by some to be poetical, by others to be unnatural. It is certainly capable of poetical treatment and feeling, but in itself is singularly prosaic. Supposing when it rained we said, Heaven is sick. This would surely not be a poetical trope, but it would be one on the exact lines of our Vedic tale. As to such a view being unnatural, do

not, O reader, fall into the absurd error of supposing
that it is unnatural, because it is not our nineteenth-
century-way of regarding the matter.   It is we who,
in a sense, are profoundly unnatural in such things.
Mr. Herbert Spencer well reminds us that 'No
servant-girl is surprised at the sun.'   Why is this?
On account of her great knowledge?   No, but because
she is used to it; and our civilization, such as it is,
has filled her head with other matters.   The archaics
often talked poetry in happy ignorance of so doing ;
the modern (so-called) poet often talks prose in the
same cheerful condition.

But how can we prove that the Vedic story does
not explain the Arkadian?   Thus.   Mannhardt says
his method of myth-interpretation is :—

   'I start from a given collection of facts, of which
the central idea is distinct and generally admitted,
and consequently offers a firm basis for explanation.
I illustrate from this and from well-founded analogies.
Continuing from these, I seek to elucidate darker
things' (Vide *M. M.*, p. 46).   An admirable principle; let us apply it here.

XII. The Dêmêter-Erinnys Myth not a dawn-tale

The 'central idea' of the Dêmêter-Erinnys legend
is that it is a tale about a Sea-god and an
Earth-goddess.   If anyone denies this, we can have
no common basis on which to discuss the matter.
But, this fact being so, how can any dawn-myth
possibly explain the story?   Prof. Müller, as of
course, strongly feels the difficulty, and makes the
only suggestion possible from his standpoint, viz.,
that for some unknown reason or other, a dawn-tale

has got entangled in the black garment of the Earth-goddess. His words are :—

' What remains but to admit that the story of the horse was told originally of another goddess,' *i.e.*, of a Dawn-goddess. 'I know this will sound very unlikely to Greek scholars [and to everybody else], yet I see no other way out of our [no,—'his'] difficulties' (*C.*, 545).

I wonder whether Prof. Müller has really convinced himself of the correctness of this suggestion. It would be idle to discuss such a bare possibility. ' Ce n'est pas dans les possibilités qu'il faut étudier l'homme,' says De Brosses. Mr. Lang naturally criticises the Professor's hypothesis, rightly in-sisting :—

' Demeter is a goddess of Earth, not of Dawn. How, then, does the explanation of a hypothetical Dawn-myth [There is no real doubt about this Vedic Dawn-myth.] apply to the earth?'

And the only answer is, The explanation cannot apply. Mannhardt, quoted by Mr. Lang (*M. M.*, pps, 52-3), pitilessly reproduces the discordant con-jectures anent the Dêmêtêr-Erinnys myth. Dêmêtêr = Storm Cloud, Sun-goddess, Earth and Moon Goddess, Dawn, Night. How wilfully Preller and the other nine sages mentioned went wrong over the matter ! They knew that Dêmêtêr was and must be the Earth-goddess. But they deliberately gave arbitrary and non-natural interpretations of her, because otherwise they felt themselves unable to suggest an explanation of the story. Better, far better, to leave it altogether unexplained than to run counter to an obvious fact. But the Natural

Phenomena Theory is not at fault, or to blame, because it is thus deliberately misapplied. The suggestions continue :—Poseidôn = Sea, Storm-god, Cloud-hidden Sun, Rain-god. Ridiculous! He is the Sea-god. All the world knows it, however certain scholars under stress of weather, produced by their own fault, may pretend to forget it. Despoina = Rain, Thunder, Moon.

'Mannhardt decides, after this exhibition of guesses, that the Demeter legends cannot be explained as refractions of any natural phenomena in the heavens' (*Ib.* p. 53).

He is perfectly right.

'He concludes that the myth of Demeter Erinnys, and the parallel Vedic story of Saranyu are "incongruous," and that neither sheds any light on the other' (*Ibid*).

This is too strong ; I have shown what light the Vedic tale really does shed upon the Arkadian legend. But the utter failure of the Aryanists in this instance, does not touch either their general method, or its successful application in numberless cases. How vastly different are these mere conjectures, most of them children of despair, from the logical, well-worked-out, harmonious theory which culminates in such a equation as Ahanâ = Athêna.

XIII. Real Character of the Dêmêtêr-Erinnys Myth

Is, then, this singular Dêmêtêr-Erinnys myth insoluble? Not so. *It is a non-Aryan myth ;* that's all. Aryan dawn-stories, therefore, will not help us. The Sea-and-horse god Poseîdôn is a non-Aryan divinity. But, the reader will exclaim, Surely

Dêmêtêr is an Aryan goddess. Undoubtedly ; I
have already said as much (Vide *sup.* p. 20). But,
know, O vain man, that to assume that in Hellenic
regions an Aryan name necessarily covers an Aryan
divinity has led to very grave errors. Let me
illustrate. One of the *Homilies* speaks of Juno as a
goddess of that great Phoenician city Qarth-hadasth
(= Carthada, Solinus ; Lat. Carthago ; Eng. Carthage, *i.e.*, ' the New Town.'). Every scholar knows
that, *verbatim et literatim*, this is absurd. He also
knows that what is meant is, that there was a
Carthaginian goddess whom the Romans regarded as
the equivalent of the Latin Juno. Or, again, take
the case of Hêra Akraia at Korinth. Such a careful
and well-informed writer as Mr. Farnell is perfectly
aware that she is not the Aryan spouse of Zeus, but
a Phoenician goddess (Vide *Cults*, i. 201 *et seq.*).
And so, when a Semitic Earth-goddess has penetrated
into the Peloponnêsos, the Greeks, according to
their constant practice, bestow upon her the name
of their own Earth-goddess. And when once we
take this standpoint, every incident in the strange
description of the goddess, her unanthropomorphic
form, her horse's head, cave, serpents, wild beasts,
black garment, dolphin and dove, and the place
Onkeion, all alike become luminous, because all alike
are Semitic traits (Vide Bérard, *Cultes Arcad.*, p. 104
et seq.). Poseidôn in name, in mythic position, in
form, is utterly non-Aryan. As the Black Goddess
is unanthropomorphic, so is he. We can see to-day
an archaic representation of him, half man, half fish,
preserved in the museum of the Akropolis. We
can see him so figured on vases, on the coins of
Phoenicia, and on the seals of Babylonia, Êa-Dagôn,

the Fish-god (Vide *inf.* pp. 102, 192). The Greek divinities, as I long ago endeavoured to show (Vide R. B. Jr., *Poseidón*, 1872) are essentially anthropomorphic. This Sea-god and Earth-goddess are not. We need not hold with Prof. Müller :—

'Here we see that Greek art shared in its beginnings the [unanthropomorphic] failings of other arts, whether Egyptian, Babylonian, or Indian' (*C.*, p. 538).

We have no Greek art in question ; the art of these two representations is Phoiniko-Babylonian. If it be objected that it is a far cry from Babylonia to Arkadia, I rejoin that it is a still farther cry to India. It is a far cry from Babylon to St. Andrews, yet the good folks of that place divide their time-calculation into sixty seconds make a minute, sixty minutes make an hour, simply because thousands of years ago the Babylonians adopted a sexagesimal notation. I do not here enter further into the details of the story, *e.g.*, the Onkaion as connected with the Phoenician goddess of Thebes, called Athênê Onka (Cf. Paus. IX. xii. 2), and thus on. M. Bérard has treated it at great length. I wish now merely to show (1) That the Aryanistic Natural Phenomena explanations of the myth are baseless ; and (2) That this circumstance in no way affects the general application of the Natural Phenomena Theory, or the general theory of Prof. Müller ; and also to indicate (3) That the myth is non-Aryan in origin, and that the originals of Poseidôn and this 'Black (so-called) Dêmêtêr' are the Euphratean Êa, Lord of the Deep (which includes the sea), and his consort the Earth-goddess Davkina ('Lady-of-the-Earth ').

XIV. Mannhardt on the Demeter-Erinnys Myth

Mannhardt was a great student. He busied himself alike with the anthropological and the natural-
phenomena aspect of mythology; and consequently
is claimed by both camps as an ally. But there is
really nothing to dispute about; one side of his shield
was golden, the other silver. Evidently disgusted
by the baseless Aryanistic speculations anent the
myth, he plunges into an opposite extreme. His
excruciating etymology of so simple a name as
Dêmêtêr has already been mentioned (Vide *sup.*
p. 16) ; and he proceeds to tackle the tale thus (Vide
M. M. p. 51) :—

'Poseidôn is the lord of wind and wave.' So far
as the wind is concerned, this proposition is far too
broad (Vide Gladstone, *Juventus Mundi*, pp. 244-5).
'There are waves of corn, under the wind. When
the Swabian rustic sees the waves running over the
corn, he says, *Da lauft das Pferd*, and Greeks before
Homer would say, in face of the billowing corn,
There run horses.' They might, or they might not.
'And Homer says that the horses of Erichthonius,
children of Boreas [*i.e.*, the Winds], ran over cornfield and sea.' Yes; but Poseidôn is not the Wind
or winds, so that he is unconnected with these
children of Boreas. As some of those at whom he
laughs make Poseidôn (the Sea-god) into the sun;
so Mannhardt, under similar stress from *his* theory,
makes him into the wind. Had it been Hermês,
there might have been something plausible to be
said for this idea. Mannhardt quotes some more
'peasant proverbs,' but they are not Arkadian
proverbs, and they were not said of Poseidôn. We

4

must stick to the story. If we allow that the Sea-god was the Wind, how can we object to the view that he was the Sun. The sun (Iasiôn) does marry the cultivated earth (Dêmêtêr) ; the wind does not. And yet Mannhardt can conclude :—

' It is a probable hypothesis [Observe, even the author of it can put it no higher.] that the belief in the wedding of Demeter and Poseidon comes from the sight of the waves passing over the cornfield.'

' It is very neat,' says Mr. Lang. But he doesn't believe it, and right he is. What becomes, on these lines, of the Twins? If the wind bowing the grain reminds us of a horse, why should the grain itself remind us of a mare? How does the wind follow and wed corn, and make it yield increase? How is corn, in any sense, draped in black? How does Mannhardt explain the Onkaion, or the peculiar statue of the goddess with her symbols and adjuncts? He can't explain one of these things. His 'hypothesis,' as he calls it, is more utterly and obviously baseless than any one of those which he condemns, a circumstance which shows how infinitely easier it is to criticise than to create. Says Mr. Lang :—

' A certain myth of Loki in horse-form comes into memory, and makes me wonder how Mannhardt would have dealt with that too literal narrative.'

And he slyly adds :—

' Is Loki a corn-spirit ? '

Umps ! ' The rest is silence.'

A verbal point in the tale remains for notice. As we have seen, the Arkadians used the word 'ερυνύειν (= ' To-act-like-an-Erînys ') colloquially in the sense of 'to-be-in-a-fury.' Some wonderful philologists, opponents of Prof. Müller, have actually derived Ἐρινύς (a 'Fury') from 'ἐρινύειν, an admirable instance of *Hysteron-proteron*, or the cart before the horse. How anyone could be said 'to-act-like-a-Fury' before Furies had been thought of, does not appear. I suppose we shall be told ere long that 'critic' is derived from the verb 'to criticise,' and that Mausôlos obtained his name from his mausoleum. I have omitted to notice a 'guess' of Mr. Lang anent the Horse-Dêmêtêr. 'The gods in savage myths are usually beasts. As beasts they beget anthropomorphic offspring. This is the regular rule in totemism.' (*M. M.* p. 68). Quite so. But Poseidôn was ignorant of this rule, and so begat a horse, Areiôn.

XV. A 'Disease of Language'

Says Prof. Müller :—

'The question of mythology has become in fact a question of psychology.'

This circumstance, of course, gives it its great interest and importance.

'As our psyche becomes objective to us chiefly through language' mythology has become 'a question of the science of language. This will explain why, when trying to explain the inmost nature of mythology, I called it a Disease of Language rather than of Thought.'

He admits that the expression was 'startling,' but thinks it has done good, and continues :—

'After I had [rightly or wrongly] fully explained in my Science of Thought that language and thought are inseparable, and that a disease of language is

4 *

therefore the same as a disease of thought, no doubt
ought to have remained as to what I meant' (*C.*
pp. 68-9).

He explains that he was thinking of far more than
mere misapprehensions, *e.g.*, taking ' μῆλα, flocks, for
μῆλα, apples,' or than false etymology, wrong pronunciation, and ' similar accidents.' He meant to
refer to that state of language and thought which
represents ' the Supreme God as committing every
kind of crime,'—which, in fact, puzzles us, by pre-
senting to us extraordinary tales about the divinities.
These stories, which much tormented some ancient
Greek thinkers, it·is impossible to take *literatim et
verbatim*. They must therefore contain a Hyponoia,
an Undermeaning. But what is this? Now I quite
admit that the expression 'disease of language,'
' disease of thought,' is not a happy one. Prof.
Müller quotes ' Mr. Horatio Hale, the Nestor of
scientific ethnologists,' who writes :—

' The expression " a disease of language " was too
sweeping, but it comprises a large measure of truth.'

Mr. Lang, as might be expected, pounces upon
this phrase ; and, *more suo*, makes an exquisite
pleasantry touching the measles, which will probably
be thought a perfect side-splitter by Those-who-go-
into-these-things-a-little (Vide *sup.* p. 33). Dis-
regarding the Professor's explanation that, in his
terminology, 'disease of language' = 'disease of
thought,' Mr Lang again and again represents Prot.
Müller as teaching that language, as distinct from
thought, and 'especially language in a state of
" disease " ' has ' been the great source of the mytho-

logy of the world' (*M. M.* p. x). That which I
understand Prof. Müller to mean by the expressions
'disease' of language or of thought, is what I should
rather call the outcome of a failure of memory, such
failure being intensified by the ever shifting significa-
tions of words. Illustrations will make clearer the
views of Prof. Müller and Mr. Lang on the matter.
Says the latter :—

'To me, and indeed to Mr. Max Müller, the ugly
scars [= The extraordinary stories of mythology.]
were the problem . . . The phenomena which the
philological school of mythology explains by a disease
of language we ['Untutored' or 'Unawakened' Anthropologists, I presume.] would explain by survival
from a savage state of society and from the mental
peculiarities observed among savages' (*M. M.* p. 5).

Very well. So long as these phenomena are really
explained, let the instrument be what it may. We
will take an 'ugly-scar'-tale :—Isis and Osiris were
linked in love in their mother's womb (Vide Renouf,
Rel. Anct. Egypt, p. 111). Now, Open Sesame!

Is such a little incident common to 'a savage state
of society,' and therefore one which naturally arises
in the mind of a tale-inventor? Or, if not, what are
'the mental peculiarities observed among savages'
which cause such an idea? The comparative mythologist, the disciple of the Natural Phenomena Theory,
says, and, notwithstanding Mr. Frazer (Vide *sup.*
p. 14), with the support of Egyptologists, that Isis
(Dawn) and Osiris (Sun), regarded as a harmonious
pair, are hidden together in the womb of Night. The
story is neither silly nor filthy. It merely results
from the fact that archaic man, and herein much re-

sembling modern man, measured all things by himself,
and regarded what he saw from an anthropomorphic
point of view. The 'ugly scars' disappear. The
last part of Mr. Lang's sentence is very elastic; and
if he should chance to mean that this anthropomorph-
ism is amongst 'the mental peculiarities' of modern
savages, then he would probably be really more in
agreement with Prof. Müller than he supposes.

So, in innumerable myths, which, when regarded
as relating doings such as those of human beings,
involve gods and heroes in every species of cruelty
and immorality, the scars will at once disapper when
we realize that man is talking, in anthropomorphic
language, of the phenomena, celestial or otherwise, of
the world around, as they strike upon his conscious-
ness. But, as the years roll on, the original meaning
of the sacred old tale fades away, whilst the words
remain, the shell is carefully preserved. We are left
with a letter which kills, and deprived of a spirit
which gives life; and the ultimate result is practically
a disease alike of language and of thought. That
this process has actually been passed through by man,
has been demonstrated by mythologists in hundreds
of instances. That numbers of such stories cannot
possibly be explained by savage states of society, or
by the mental peculiarities of modern savages, I have
just shown and will show again (Vide *inf.* p. 73).

XVI. Alleged Egyptian Totemism

Mr. Lang gives a careful and valuable definition of
Totemism :—

'A state of society and cult, found most fully
developed in Australia and North America, in which

sets of persons, believing themselves to be akin by
blood, call each such set by the name of some plant,
beast, or other class of objects in nature.' To its
beast, etc. each kin pays ' more or less respect [This
is elastic.], usually abstains from killing, eating, or
using it (except in occasional sacrifices) ; is apt to
claim descent from or relationship with it,' and
' uses its effigy ' in various ways (*M. M.* p. 71).

As archaic Egypt furnishes us with an example of
various sacred animals and of gods in animal form,
it presents a tempting field for annexation by the
Totemist. On this point Prof. Müller observes :—

' It might be possible to explain every kind of ther-
iolatry by totemism. Why should not all the gods
of Egypt with their heads of bulls, and apes and cats
be survivals of totemism? But though it would
relieve Egyptologists of a great difficulty, none of the
leading hieroglyphic scholars seems as yet to have
availed himself of this remedy ' (*C.* p. 202).

To this Mr. Lang practically replies as did Panurge
to Master Rondibilis, ' There did I wait for you,'
saying :—

' Mr. Max Müller asks if " any Egyptologists have
adopted " the totem theory. He is apparently
oblivious of Professor Sayce's reference to a pre-
historic age, " when the religious creed of Egypt
was still totemism" ' (*M. M.* p. 72. Vide Sayce, *Herod.*
p. 344. Mr. Lang does not give the reference).

Mr. Lang further quotes Robertson Smith, who
states that :—

' In Egypt the gods themselves are totem-deities,
i.e., personifications or individual representations of

the sacred character and attributes which in the purely totem stage of religion were ascribed without distinction to all animals of the holy kind' (Vide *M. M.* p. 76).

And here I will make Mr. Lang a present of another quotation from Prof. Sayce, who, speaking of the Babylonian Istar-Gilgames myth, says :—

'Here popular tradition has preserved a recollection of the time when the gods of Babylonia were still regarded as eagles, and horses, and lions. We are taken back to an epoch of totemism, when the tribes and cities of Chaldæa had each its totem, or sacred animal, to whom it offered divine worship, and who eventually became its creator-god' (*Rel. Anct. Babs.* p. 279).

Mr. Lang concludes :—

'Robertson Smith and Mr. Sayce are " scholars," not mere unscholarly anthropologists' (*M. M.* p. 76).

Now let it be granted, for the sake of argument, that Robertson Smith and my friend Prof. Sayce, are absolutely correct in the above statements. We are all aware that Prof. Sayce, of whom I speak with the utmost respect, has a great knowledge of Egypt, ancient and modern. But would he style himself an 'Egyptologist'? I think not. Robertson Smith certainly was not an Egyptologist.

Next, what is it exactly that Robertson Smith and Prof. Sayce affirm in these quotations? Do they attribute to archaic Egypt and Chaldaea totemism on the lines of Mr. Lang's definition? Most certainly not. Do they state that there was a time in archaic Egypt and Chaldaea when a distinct set of persons

inhabited each nome or district, believed themselves
to be akin by blood, called each such set by the
name of their totem-plant, beast, etc., abstained from
killing, etc. such totem, and claimed descent from
or relationship with it? They do not; nor is there
any evidence that such a state of things ever existed.
They merely use the words 'totem,' 'totemism,' in
a somewhat vague and general sense.   Thus,
Prof. Sayce defines his Chaldaean totem as a 'sacred
animal'; but, as Mr. Lang well observes:—

'Animal attributes, and symbols, and names in
religion are not necessarily totemistic' (*M. M.* p. 72).

The fact is that Mr. Lang has incautiously applied
his definition of totemism, in all its rigour, to the
statements of these two scholars ; and has assumed
that, when they spoke of totemism, they imagined it
thus.   And to return to the statement of Prof.
Müller.   Not one undoubted Egyptologist from
Champollion down to Maspero and De Morgan is a
believer in Egyptian totemism.   Lastly, it is clear
from Strabo (xvii. 40) that all Egypt worshipped
the ox, cat, hawk, and ibis; therefore there were no
totem clans (properly so-called) in the country.
Result:—Exit totemism from the Nile Valley.

XVII.   Another instance of exploded Totemism

In his *Custom and Myth*, 1st edit. p. 119, note,
Mr. Lang says:—

'Though Plutarch mentions an Athenian γένος,
the Ioxidæ, which claimed descent from and revered
asparagus, it is probable that genuine totemism had

died out of Greece many hundreds of years before even Homer's time.'

He again (p. 264) recurs to this extraordinary statement, which he was very fond of introducing when reviewing books, and remarks :—

' We know from Plutarch that, in addition to families claiming descent from divine animals, one Athenian γένος, the Ioxidæ, revered an ancestral plant, the asparagus.'

This was indeed an admirable instance in illustration of Mr. Lang's totemistic theories. There was only a single jar about it, but that was rather a nasty one. Plutarch says nothing of the kind. In 1884 I pointed out this fact in the *Academy* ; and Mr. Lang has since withdrawn the statement. But it is very needful to verify quotations ; for, as we shall again have opportunity of observing, the enthusiastic Totemist's eyesight often deceives him.

XVIII. Apollôn, Mr. Lang, and the Mouse

In his *Custom and Myth*, Mr. Lang has an amusing article called *Apollo and the Mouse*. It dealt with the cult of Apollôn Smintheus, σμίνθος being a local name in the Troad for a mouse ; and endeavoured to prove the existence of a mouse-totem in regions Hellenic. In support of this theory Mr. Lang explored Egypt, but found, on the authority of Prof. Sayce, that ' mice were not sacred in Egypt.' But, if we cannot catch a mouse, let us get a rat ; and says Mr. Lang :—

' Rats, however, were certainly sacred, and as little

distinction is taken, in myth, between rats and mice as between rabbits and hares. The rat was sacred to Ra, the Sun-god, and (like all totems) was not to be eaten ' (*Custom and Myth*, 2nd edit. revised, p. 113).

Wilkinson (*Ancient Egyptians*, iii. 294) is quoted in support of this statement. I refer thither, but find nothing to the effect that the rat is sacred. But I do find (p. 259) the rat tabled as ' Not sacred.' I protest, as Mr. Lang and Tommy Merton would say, I cannot understand this. And in the ' revised ' edition too! Mr. Lang refers to the *Book of the Dead*, cap. xxxiii, to show that the rat was ' sacred to Ra.' But the passage in question (ap. Renouf) reads:—

' Stop! or thou shalt eat the rat which Rā execrateth, and gnaw the bones of a putrid she-cat.'

It is quite clear that the execrable rat and ' putrid she-cat ' were not sacred to Râ, the Sun-god. The Rat thus refused to come to Mr. Lang's assistance against his fellow the Mouse, and the latter strongly objected to be made into a totem. Mr. Lang, however, had found six ' notes' (Vide *M. M.* p. 80) which seemed to point to a Greek mouse-totem ; and, emboldened by apparent success, had applied similar arguments to the Bear, the Bull, and the Pig, ' and so forth.'

XIX.   Rout of Mr. Lang by the Mouse

Says Mr. Lang :—

' My theory connecting Apollo Smintheus . . . . with a possible [All things out of the mathematics are possible.] pre-historic mouse-totem, gave me, I confess, considerable satisfaction ' (*Ib.* p. 84).

But, at this juncture the Mouse, still desperately resisting, found an unexpected ally in no less a person than Mr. Frazer, armed with his *Golden Bough*. Mr. Frazer showed, what indeed various ancient writers had showed before him, that ' mice and other vermin are worshipped for prudential reasons —to get them to go away.' Mr. Ward Fowler, in the *Classical Review*, was of the same opinion. So also were Strabo and Pausanias (Vide *inf.* p. 211), though Mr. Lang had not noticed their opinions until too late. The Mouse,—it must have ' Lick-man,' named in the *Batrachomyomachia*,—placing himself at the head of this phalanx, bore down with redoubled energy upon Mr Lang, who (small blame to him) turned and fled. When he recovered breath he said :—

' Apollo may be connected with mice, not as a god who superseded a mouse-totem, but as an expeller of mice, like the worm-killing Heracles, and the Locust-Heracles, and the Locust-Apollo. Thus the Mouse-Apollo (Smintheus) would be merely a god noted for his usefulness in getting rid of mice, and any worship given to mice . . . would be mere acts of propitiation. There would be no mouse-totem in the back-ground.'

Just so. Mr. Lang, however, does not ' feel quite convinced—the mouse being a totem . . . in Egypt.' But, as we have seen (*Sup.* p. 58), it wasn't. Our Author consoles himself by rejecting Grohmann's dogma that the Mouse is 'the Lightning '; and surely this proposition is not of faith, but of pious opinion. I confess I think that one of this triad, Apollôn,

Mr. Lang, and the Mouse looks somewhat 'ridiculous.'
Apollôn is untouched, and the Mouse victorious.
But all honour to Mr. Lang for recognising the force
of the hostile evidence, and admitting that anthropologists, as well as philologists and politicians may
be great at leaps in the dark.   Mere ordinary Philis-
tines, especially those residing at Ashqelôn, Gaza,
Ekron, Ashdod, and Gath, have known the truth all
along (Vide 1 *Sam.* vi).

XX. Artemis, Arkas and the Bear

Deprived of his totem-mouse Mr. Lang sadly
exclaims :—

'I do hanker after the Arcadian bear as, at least, a
possible survival of totemism . . . Will Mr. Frazer
give the Arcadian bear "the benefit of the doubt?"'
(*M. M.* p. 87).

'I am not sure that the corn-spirit accounts for
the Sminthian mouse in all his aspects, nor for the
Arcadian and Attic bear-rites and myths of Artemis.
Mouse and bear do appear in Mr. Frazer's catalogue
of forms of the corn-spirits, taken from Mannhardt'
(*Ibid.*).

This is a very just scepticism. The Corn-spirit
threatens to extend his ravages even into districts
where there is no corn.

'But the Arcadians, as we shall see, *claimed
descent* from a bear' (*Ibid.*).

This we shall not see, for they made no such claim.
What says Pausanias? Why that Arkas (probably
a Ph. name. Cf. Ph. Arci, now Arkos, in Spain; the
Archites, *Jos.* xvi. 2 ; etc.) introduced the sowing of

corn, and taught his people how to make bread and weave and other things, and that in his reign the country was called Arkadia instead of Pelasgia and the inhabitants Arkadians instead of Pelasgians (Paus. VIII. iv. 1). The Arkadians were not descended from Arkas, even as the English are not descended from Alfred. These unfortunate errors in fact on the part of Mr. Lang, arising from carelessness and ' smattering,' cause a just suspicion of his quotations and general statements.

Next, as to Arkas himself. Was he said to be simply and actually the child of a bear? *Distinguo,* as Mr. Lang would say. The Arkadian legend spoke of him as the child of a ' Most-beautiful ' (Kallistô) woman, who, after he had been begotten, was changed into a bear. And notwithstanding this alleged metamorphosis the Greek mind continued to regard Kallistô as a woman, not as a bear; and it is as a woman that she appeared alike on the coinage of Arkadia and on the canvas of Polygnôtos, though in the latter instance accompanied by her bear-skin. Whatever may have been the origin of all this, surely it is quite distinct from Totemism as (very properly) defined by Mr. Lang. The Arkadians did not claim descent from a bear, did not call themselves ' bears '; in a word, did not fulfil those necessary conditions which mark the real Totemist. Truly there was a certain connexion between them and bears. Until quite late times the animal was found in the country (Cf. Paus. VIII. xxiii. 6); and they were acquainted with the constellations of the *Great* and *Little Bear.*

Prof. Müller deals with the story at length, but not happily; and this circumstance arises, as we shall see, from his mythological standpoint. Mr. Lang quotes the Professor's remarks (*M. M.* p. 137 *et seq.*) and criticises his 'explanation.' I doubt whether Prof. Müller gives any explanation. He suggests that ' Arcas reminded the Arcadians of *arktos.*' If it did, we shall never know the fact. I shall, with the assistance of Bachofen and M. Victor Bérard, whose work *De l'Origine des Cultes Arcadiens* (1894), is one of the finest specimens of ' modern mythology,' place another interpretation on the legend.

The learned and sober researches of Bachofen, *Der Baer in den Religionen des Alterthums*, 1863, who has carefully examined most. of the instances in classical literature where the bear is referred to, or where bear-names occur, and who also gives various illustrations of the bear in classical art, furnish the following result:—

The Ancients were greatly struck, not so much by the size, etc., of the animal, as by her extraordinary affection for her young; and attributed to her strange and special powers of licking them into shape, etc. Briefly, the maternal, and hence fostering and kindly, aspect of the Bear, which in Greek is always feminine, ἡ Ἄρκτος, 'the fem. being used even when both sexes are included' (Liddell and Scott, *in voc.*), is the leading idea in the mythologico-religious treatment of the animal. The Semitic world equally appreciated this same characteristic, as, *e.g.*, divers Biblical proverbialisms show; and the bear of the shores of the Mediterranean stands before us as *Ursa Matronalis*, a symbol of that fostering love which will do and dare all on behalf of the objects of its affection. Such an animal naturally became connected with the cult of the great non-Aryan Goddess-mother of Western Asia

(Cf. Lucian, *Peri tês Syriês Theou,* xli.; Renan, *Phenicie,* p. 292; O. Keller, *Thiere des klassisch. Alterth.* pp. 106-128; Bérard, *Cultes Arcad.* p. 130; etc.). According to Porphyry (*Pythagorou Bios,* xli.) Pythagoras, who was a native of Samos, a locality famous for the worship of the Great Goddess, whom there the Hellenes, not unnaturally, identified with their Hêra, speaking 'symbolically and in mystic fashion,' calls bears, ' the hands (*i.e.*, assistants) of Rhea' (τὰς ἄρκτους 'Ρέας χεῖρας), meaning apparently that they were exemplars and supporters of the *dignitas matronalis.* And this leads us directly to Helikê (*Ursa Major*) and Kynosoura (*Ursa Minor*). For, when Rhea was about to give birth to Zeus, she retired to Kretan Lyktos, and hid the infant in a cave (Hêsiod, *Theog.* 477-84), where he was nurtured by two bears. And Aratos (*Phainom.* 31-5), repeating the ancient story from Agaosthenês of Naxos, identifies this pair with the constellation-bears. All, or nearly all, of the mythological stories about the bear, show the animal in the same kindly light, and frequently in a Semitic connexion. A bear suckles Atalantê, in whom 'nous retrouvions tous les attributs de la déesse syrienne' (Bérard, *Cultes Arcad.* p. 131). Long ago Otfried Müller showed that Kallistô == Artemis Kallistê; and this latter personage is no more the Aryan sister of Apollôn than is Artemis Ephesia, but the Semitic ' Reine-Mère,' connected with a constellation (the *Wain*-stars) also called ' Most beautiful.' ' Comme le mot sémitique [*Noemâ*] dont il est la traduction, καλλίστη célèbre tout à la fois la beauté et la bonté de la désse' (*Ib.* pp. 202-3). To make the story intelligible to later ages, a strictly human element is

introduced in Euhemeristic fashion. Zeus becomes
the faithless husband, Hêra the jealous wife, Artemis
the avenging friend. But all this is merely a layer
of dust and ashes over the original facts and beliefs.
Arkas (Gk. ' The Bright-one '), son of Zeus Lykaios
(= Baal Khamman or Hamon = Gk. Palaimôn),
and the beautiful (' Kallistê ') Phoenician goddess, at
once virgin and mother, dies and comes to life again,
and also exhibits the familiar Semitic aspect of
triplicity. ' Arcas, le héros-enfant, le dieu-soleil, est
un triple dieu, l'infernal Apheidas, le céleste Elatos,
et le fort Azan' (*Ib.* p. 269). Azan, whom Pausanias
calls the eldest son of Arkas, is merely the Semitic
Sun-god as Aziz or Azan (' the Strong '). We meet
with him in Boiôtia as Azeus, in Syria as Azôn, said
to be a son of Melqârth (= Melikertês) and founder
of Aza, otherwise Gaza. Arkas naturally becomes
Arktophylax Boôtês, so well known to Homer, the
' Bearward-Ploughman,' Herdsman or Shouter—at
the Bear, who, with her Sister, guards the Pole.
The introduction of constellation-figures is alone
an almost certain indication of Semitic influence.
Mr. Lang once wrote in a magazine :—

' The Greeks received from the dateless past of
savage intellect the myths, and the names of the
constellations.'

It is perfectly easy to write imaginary history
such as this. You only require invention + pen,
ink, and paper. And statements of the kind are
doubtless quite good enough for ' the public which
" goes into these things a little " '; and, differing but
slightly from a country yokel, accepts with open
mouth almost anything it may see in print, especially

if a prominent name be attached to the statement. Mr. Lang doubtless believed what he said, and may believe it still. But it is scarcely fair to the unfortunate public to write so recklessly. As a matter of fact the Greeks received the constellation-names, which we now use, and nearly all the stories connected with them, not from any savages, but from the highly civilized Phoenicians, who, in turn, like the ancient Arabians (Vide Hommel, *Ueber den Ursprung und das Alter der arabischen Sternnamen*, 1891), had received many of these names, *e.g.*, the *Wain*, the *Goat* (*Aix-Capella*), *a Aurigae*, and the *Eagle*, from the archaic civilization of the Euphrates Valley.

And thus much touching Kallistô, the Arkadians, and the Bear.[1]

---

[1] I have for many years been engaged in collecting material for a work to be entitled *Researches into the Origin of the Primitive Constellations of the Greeks, Phoenicians, and Babylonians*. Ideler's admirable *Sternnamen* was published in 1809, and since then the subject has been almost entirely in the hands of 'smatterers,' who have naturally aired nearly every possible absurdity of assertion and conjecture. If my health permits me to finish it, I can wish no more success for this work than that it should be regarded as Ideler up to date. In a special monograph (*The Celestial Equator of Aratos*, with 33 illustrations, in the *Transactions* of the Ninth International Congress of Orientalists, London, 1892, vol. ii., pp. 445-85), I have shown that the astronomical statements preserved in the *Phainomena* of Aratos, and hitherto regarded as inexplicable, were derived from Babylonia, and were perfectly correct for that locality, cir. B.C. 2084. In *The Heavenly Display*, (Longmans, 1885) I have given the only accurate translation of the *Phainomena* (as a basis for the study of archaic astronomy) which has yet appeared in English. This work contains an Introduction, Notes, Appendices, and 68 illustrations of constellation-figures,

XXI. The Brauronian Bear-cult

We have next to deal with the bear on Attic ground. Twenty years ago I made a careful study of the Brauronian bear-cult (Vide *The Great Dionysiak Myth*, i. 239 *et seq.*; ii. 134 *et seq.*), which has recently attracted much attention in a totemistic connexion. I showed in detail how absurd it is to confound the Brauronian goddess, Artemis-Orthia (= Sem. Ashêrah, 'The Upright,' the Phoenician goddess of the phallic stone-cones)-Taurikê, with the Aryan sister of Apollôn. Although the exact reason is at times somewhat difficult to perceive, nothing is more certain than that the Greeks again and again applied the name of Artemis to foreign divinities, supposed to resemble her, more or less, the most familiar instance of which is the unanthropomorphic Polymastos of Ephesos, but the most remarkable, the Eurynomê-Derketô Artemis of Phigaleia, half-woman, half-fish. Artemis of Braurôn, like Artemis-Kallistê-Kalistô, is a Semitic divinity (Vide Bérard,

many of them taken from Euphratean Boundary-stones. In another monograph (*The Archaic Lunar Zodiac*, in the *Proceedings* of the Society of Biblical Archaeology, Dec. 1895-Jan. 1896) I have proved that the seven complete specimens of a lunar zodiac which have come down to us, viz., the Persian, Sogdian, Khorasmian, Chinese, Indian, Arab, and Coptic schemes, are all variants, and derived from a Sumero-Babylonian original. And I mention these circumstances, in order that the reader may perceive that I do not offer an opinion on questions connected with the ancient constellation-figures, without having first given long and careful attention to the subject. If therefore he should hear my views treated with contempt and merely asserted to be baseless, let him remember to take such 'criticism' at its proper value. He will not meet with any *refutation* of my general position.

5 *

Cultes Arcad. pp. 132-3) bearing an Aryan goddess-name, and actually a patroness of the bear (Vide *sup.* Sec. xx). Mr. Lang truly says that his account of the Brauronian ritual is inferior to that of Mr. L. R. Farnell, whose *Cults of the Greek States* (1896), only the two first volumes of which have appeared, is a work of which any scholar might well be proud. As Mr. Farnell is mainly of the same school as Mr. Lang, I will examine his view of the matter, and assail the *fort* rather than the *faible* (Vide *M. M.* p. 102). Mr. Farnell gives an excellent *résumé* of the facts :—

'We learn from Aristophanes that it was the custom for young maidens, clothed in a saffron robe, to dance in the Brauronian ceremonies of Artemis, and that in this dance they, as well as the priestess, were called " bears "; the saffron robe was possibly worn in order to imitate the tawny skin of the bear. . . The dance was called ἀρκτεία, and the maidens who took part in it were between five and ten years of age. . . The scholiast says that Artemis ordered every maiden [for a reason given]. . . to dance the bear-dance before marriage and to pass round the temple wearing the saffron robe. . . The dance was a kind of initiation by which young girls before arriving at puberty were consecrated to the goddess ' (*Cults*, ii. 436-7).

Mr. Farnell, who regards Braurônis as the Aryan Artemis, next states that ' the goddess and her worshippers and the bear were considered as of one nature.' This is only true in so far as they all were representatives of feminality. He then introduces divers ' totemistic illustrations,' to which I beg the

reader's careful attention. According to proper
totemistic principles, a bear ought to have been
' offered in a sacrificial meal to the goddess on solemn
occasions.' Unfortunately, however, these regulations
were grossly violated ; as ' the authorities make it
clear that a goat or hind was usually the animal of
sacrifice.' He proceeds :—

' The substitution of the goat for the bear '—

Stop! Stop! My good sir; you have not yet
proved that a bear ever was sacrificed on the occasion, so how could there be a ' substitution of the
goat'? But let this pass. ' The substitution of the
goat for the bear was a violation of the logic of the
ceremony.' Shocking! Especially since the fact
gives a nasty jar to the totemistic theorist. Take
courage, however, and we shall get over this. Bears,
it seems, were scarce. The little maidens would
have sacrificed them, if they could have caught any.
But Pausanias (I. xxxii. 1) says there were bears, in
his time, on Mount Parnês, not very far off; and the
Arkadian oak-groves still sheltered them. Moreover,
as he remarks (VIII. xvii. 3), private individuals have
before now brought white bears from Thrace, but
then white was not the right colour for Braurôn.
Mr. Farnell's last suggestion in explanation of this
' logical' difficulty anent the sacrifice is quite worthy
of Prof. Aguchekikos himself. Perhaps, he surmises,
' chance may here have put the ritual into the hands of
a goat-tribe.' It would be well first to show that there
really were any Bear-tribes or Goat-tribes in the
locality. And it is truly instructive to what straits
the logical application of unsound premisses will
reduce a very able man.

Avoiding all such totemistic imaginings, we see at a glance how exactly the Brauronian ritual harmonizes with the views of Bachofen and M. Bérard. Each little Attic maid, as a representative of feminality, is solemnly dedicated to the goddess connected alike with virginity and with motherhood. And as the Bear, regarded as *Ursa Matronalis*, is sacred to this Artemis, strangely unlike the virgin sister of Apollôn, so these maidens, the matrons of the future, are her bears. How simple it all really is! And it will be observed that the bear-maidens passed 'round the temple,' just as the celestial Kallistô passes slowly round the sacred spot occupied by the Pole-star, called in Akkadian *Tir-anna*, = Bab.-As. *Dayan-samê* (' Judge-of-heaven ') ; so that the dance, like many others, may have been connected with, and, to some extent, imitative of, the eternal choric stellar dance, which ' the moving gems of night,' as Aratos calls them, ever perform around the central and highest throne.

But, alas, for poor Mr. Lang ! Mr. Frazer's encroaching Corn-spirit has frightened away his Totem-pig and Totem-bull (Vide *M. M.* p. 86). The Mouse, as we have seen, would have none of him. And now, saddest of all, the Totem-bear vanishes ; and, like the objectionable Apparition which annoyed Lord Lyttleton, leaves him in a similarly melancholy solitude. Well might he exclaim : —

> I never loved a totem-mouse,
> And trained it through my books to follow ;
> But it would vanish from my house
> Of cards, and leave me with Apollo.

I hankered for a totem-bear,—
Found one exactly to my mind ;
When, lo ! it disappeared in air,
And left but Artemis behind ! [1]

This is all very sad. Let us pass on.

XXII. A Key of Knowledge from Mr. Lang's Bunch

Mr. Lang is only occasionally constructive. On the whole it suits him better to carry on a light guerilla warfare against the *faible* rather than against

---

[1] The Aryan name Ἄρτεμις, Dor. Ἄρταμις, has never yet been satisfactorily explained. We may gather from the general concept of the goddess, that it will probably be some simple epithet of the moon. Let us consider it on these lines. We find the Aryan roots *ar* and *ri*, meaning ' to go '; from the former comes the Arian form *arta*, ' right,' *i.e.*, ' going on straight,' and the Avestic ' *aretha* (*ar* + *rta*, ἄρετη ?), ce qui va droit; justice, droit ' (De Harlez, *Manuel de la Langue de l'Avesta*, p. 119). *Arta* appears in many Persian proper names (Vide Canon Rawlinson, *Herod.* iii. 445); and is at times regarded as having an intensitive force, *e.g.*, Pers. *Arta-syras*, = ' the Very-Bright' or ' the Bright-sun.' From the root *ri* is formed the Vedic *rita*, meaning primarily ' the straight line '; then, what is straight, fixed, permanent, right, luminous, divine law, kosmic order, etc. We find as a man's name *Rita*-bhâga= Gk.—Per. Ἀρταβάζης. So far, then, in Gk. ἄρτε, ἄρτα we obtain the ideas of going, brightness, rectitude, purity, and order. Μις is simply the Gk. μείς, μής ' month,' ' visible part of the moon,' Sk. *mas*, ' moon.' Ἄρταμις is primarily merely ' the Going-moon,' just as the Moon is called Ἰώ (' the Goer '); but she becomes the kosmic, pure (hence virgin), bright Moon of eternal law and order; who, like the Ôrîôn-sun, hunts through the halls of heaven, and bears her crescent-bow and arrows of light. And for the word μις at the end of a moon-name, we have an exact parallel in the Sk. frequent moon-name *Chandra-mas* (' Glittering-moon '). If *arta* here has merely an intensitive force, then **Arta-mis** as a moon-name, exactly corresponds with Arta-syras (= Sûrya), as a sun-name.

the *fort* of his opponents. But at times he tries his hand as a master-builder, and *e.g.*, in the case of ' the Myth of Fire-stealing,' purports to supply us with a valuable method by which to crack that often extremely hard nut, the Hyponoia of mythology. Says he :—

' The world-wide myth explaining how man first became possessed of fire—namely, by *stealing* it—might well serve as a touchstone of the philological and anthropological methods ' (*M. M* p. 193).

Very well, so be it. He then collates various interesting myths of fire-stealing, including of course the Prométheus-story ; and complains that Prof. Müller does not attempt to explain why ' Prométheus stole fire.' Lastly, he deals with this difficult problem :—

' The myth arose from the nature of savage ideas, not from unconscious puns.' ' Suppose that an early savage loses his seed of fire. His nearest neighbours, far enough off, may be hostile. If he wants fire, as they will not give it, he must *steal* it, just as he must steal a wife ' (*Ib.* p. 197).

' O hard condition ! ' well may we here exclaim. As the unfortunate man is thus compelled to steal fire, so, when he sits down and amuses himself with inventing tales, his heroes must act as he does. And Mr. Lang illustrates his view by a very singular instance of survival ;—

' If a foreign power wants what answers among us to the exclusive possession of fire, or wants the secret of its rival's new explosive, it has to *steal* it ' (*Ib.* p. 198).

Prométheus up to date! And I did not even know this. What a thing it is to be behind the scenes.

XXIII.   Application of this Method to the Myth of the Birth of Athêna

'Bravo!' cried I, on reading the foregoing explanation, 'this is better than totem bears and mice.' Here we are indeed 'on terra-cotta,' as the old lady said when she landed at Dover. And, as there is a certain mythic connexion between Prometheus and Athêna, I passed on to the latter, and hastened to try Mr. Lang's patent method upon her, beginning with the quaint myth of her birth. We know how the philological adherents of the Natural Phenomena Theory explain this. Hêphaistos (= Sk. Yavishtha, Lat. Juvenis, the ever-young Fire-power, as the Morning-sun) strikes with his axe the forehead of Zeus (= Sk. Dyaus, the Bright-sky), and up starts Athêna (= Sk. Ahanâ, the Dawn) in strength, arousing the thousand sounds and voices of the morning, Pallas (Brandishing the shafts of light), Promachos (First in the battle with Darkness), and so on. I am free to confess, as the expression is, that I have always thought (and think) this an admirable explanation of the tale, devoid alike of brutality, folly, and arbitrary invention; and one in which the philology and the details of the myth exhibit an excellent harmony. But let that pass. I observe, after reading Mr. Lang's explanation of the Fire-stealing myth, that, instead of all this, I ought to look out for some savage tribe where they have a pleasant custom of assisting a man in bringing forth a daughter by splitting open his head with an

axe. And I grieve to say that in spite of the careful attention I have bestowed upon the works of McLennan,
Robertson Smith, Mannhardt, Dr. Tylor, Mr. Lang
and others, I have not yet happened upon these
people. That there must be some such folk I feel
sure is as certain as the fall of the image of ' Diana of
the Ephesians '; and I am as honestly anxious to
encounter them as ever was Mrs. Jiniwin to behold the
body of Mr. Quilp. I can, however, at present only
say, as Mr. Brass observed on that memorable
occasion, ' We have nothing for it but resignation ;
nothing but resignation, and expectation.'

XXIV. The Sin of the god Zu

Pondering upon my disappointment, I felt a doubt
invade my soul whether after all Mr. Lang's explanation of the Fire-stealing myth would hold water.
He certainly quotes Homer on the matter, who
says :—

' As when a man hath hidden away a brand in the
black embers at an upland farm, one that hath no
neighbours nigh, and so saveth the seed of fire, that
he may not have to seek a light otherwhere, even
so' etc. (*Od.* v. 488-93, ap. Butcher and Lang).
But this good man was clearly under no necessity to
steal. From what man could the first mortal kindler
of fire have stolen it? Why must the savage always
steal fire ? Does the modern savage always steal
fire ? Was there more stealing in archaic than there
is in modern days? As all savages have fire, must
there not have been great numbers of original
archaic fire-kindlers who had no one to steal from ?
May there not be some other possible explanation of

the Fire-stealing myth, and one, moreover, independent of practical petty larceny ?

In pursuance of this train of thought, I commend to the reader's attention an archaic Euphratean story touching the god Zu. It has been translated and commented upon by Prof. Sayce (*Chaldean Account of Genesis*, 2nd edit. 1880, Cap. vii ; *Rel. Anct. Babs.*, 1887, p. 293 *et seq.*), a ' scholar,' mark ye, no ' mere unscholarly anthropologist' (Vide *M. M.* p. 76). The tale is as follows :—

To the Sumero-Akkadians 'the divine Storm-bird' was known as Lugal-tudda ('the Lusty-king '), and this concept, typified by a large bird of prey, was called by the Semitic Babylonians Zu, a word which in their language meant both a ' stormy wind ' and a kind of vulture. Into the mind of Zu entered ambition, the desire to obtain awful knowledge, and to be as the chief of the gods. According to Tablet K. No. 3454 :—

' The Tablets of Destiny, himself, Zu, he dreams of ;
He dreams that he is the Father of the gods, the protector of heaven and earth.
The desire to be Bilu (=Bel) is taken in his heart.
" Let me seize the Tablets of Destiny of the gods,
And the laws of all the gods let me establish ;
Let my throne be set up, let me seize the oracles ;
Let me urge on the whole of all of them, even the spirits of heaven." '

An opportunity occurring,

' The Tablets of Destiny he seized with his hand ;
The attributes of Bilu he took.
(Then) Zu fled away and sought his mountains.
He raised a tempest, making (a storm).'

The gods hold a council, and Anu (=Varuna-

Ouranos) asks various gods to slay Zu. They decline, but :—

'Into the Likeness of a bird was he transformed.
Into the likeness of the divine Storm-bird was he transformed,'

and banished from high heaven for ever. Prof. Sayce, after having observed that ' the conception of the tempest as a bird which rushes on its prey is common to many mythologies,' continues :—

.. 'Lugal-tudda brought the lightning, the fire of heaven, from the gods to men, giving them at once the knowledge of fire and the power of reading the future in the flashes of the storm [' To be a weather prophet was to be a prophet,' *C.* p. 76]. Like Promêtheus, therefore, he was an outcast from the gods. He had stolen their treasures and secret wisdom, and had communicated them to mankind. In Babylonia, as in Greece, the divine benefactor of primitive humanity was doomed to suffer. The knowledge and the artificial warmth man has gained are not the free gifts of the gods ; they have been wrenched from them by guile ; and though man has been allowed to retain them, his divine friend and benefactor is condemned to punishment.'

' The storm-bird, who invested himself by stealth with the attributes of Mul-lil [' Lord-of-the-Ghost-world,' from *mul*, ' lord,' + *lil*, ' ghost,' whence Heb. *Lileth*, a might-demon, cf. Is. xxxiv. 14. Mul-lil= the Semitic Bel.], and carried the knowledge of futurity to mankind, served to unite the two species of augury which read the future in the flight of birds and the flash of the lightning.'

In considering this story we cannot but be

reminded how our own Sacred Books (and sacred they are to me, however men may differ in their interpretation) connect the first catastrophe which they record with a theft of knowledge, perpetrated at the instigation of a wicked Being exiled as a rule from high heaven, although at times apparently permitted to present himself there.

The legend of Zu points not so much to petty larceny, as to the idea of larceny on a grand scale as the origin of the Fire-stealing myth ; and the form of the outcast god, fallen indeed, but still formidable in his exile and despair, is not altogether an unsuitable analogue to the Greek Fire-stealer. We can at least behold in him some faint reflection of the sombre grandeur in which the genius of Aischylos has wrapped the suffering Promêtheus.

XXV. What has Mr. Lang gained?

We are now in a position to ask, What has Mr. Lang gained by his latest 'desultory and wandering' (*M. M.* p. 200) attack upon Prof. Max Müller? Has he overthrown the Professor's philology? He does not pretend even to touch it? Has he destroyed the Natural Phenomena Theory or (so-called) Solar Mythology? On the contrary, again and again he admits that in countless instances it is, or may be, true; though he denies its application in many other cases. Has he shown that the differences of opinion amongst the adherents of Comparative Mythology are fatal to it? Only by advancing arguments which, if valid, would wreck almost every branch of knowledge; and by suppressing or ignoring the mass of instances in which philological Comparative Mythologists are agreed. Many fields

of Comparative Mythology, *e.g.*, Babylonia and
Arabia, he has not even mentioned. Has he successfully explained a single difficult myth ? Not one.
The stories of Dêmêtêr-Erinnys, Kallistô, Artemis
Braurônis, Promêtheus are beyond him. Can he
show the origin of Totemism, or preserve his totem
flock even from the ravages of Mr. Frazer's Corn-
spirit? He cannot. Pig, bull, bear, mouse, all desert
him ; and, despite a desperate effort on the part of
Mr. Farnell, Hellenic, if not Aryan, totemism like
an insubstantial pageant faded, leaves not a wrack
behind. He has much to say on 'the Question of
Allies'; and as, of course, some mythologists lean
more to philological, others to analogical, and others
to anthropological methods in their researches.
Many combine these lines, and in some instances are
allies, in others opponents. But, after all, valid
argument is better than the authority of any name
however weighty ; and both Prof. Müller and
Mr. Lang can claim powerful adherents. Mr. Lang
'smiles' when Signor Canizzaro declares, 'Lang has
laid down his arms before his adversaries'; although,
as he had for ten years 'left mythology alone'
(*M. M.* p. xxi), the error was perhaps pardonable.
And, although I tremble when I hear from Prof.
Morselli that 'Lang gives no quarter to his
adversaries,' I also smile when this same sage adds
that they 'have long been reduced to silence.'

I have not, I find, noticed a lengthy story of an
Eel and a Cocoanut, to which both Prof. Müller and
Mr. Lang have done almost more than justice. But
nothing much turns on it, the question being mainly
one touching certain real or alleged mutual misunder-
standings of each other's meaning. I therefore say

with Pausanias, ' Let these things be as they have
been from the beginning.'　An eel is but a slippery
customer at best.

And now I conclude, with Mr. Lang, ' Here ends
this " Gentle and Joyous Passage of Arms." '　As he
thus compares his effort to the tournament at Ashby,
Prof. Müller to ' the Templar,' and himself by
implication, to Ivanhoe, who upset Sir Brian, I trust
I may be allowed to observe, in the same spirit of
humility, that I felt bound to take up my axe on
behalf of the distressed damsel Comparative Mythology, whom this ' gigantic Front-de-Bœuf' (his
name declares his totemism) asserts is ' tottering,'
and to do justice upon Sir Reginald.　This done, it
only remains for me to leave him ' at the Sign of the
Ship,' a not unsuitable house of call for one who is
frequently at sea.

PART III

THE ARYO-SEMITIC SCHOOL OF HELLENIC
MYTHOLOGISTS

I. Retrospect

IN the last century, which is practically removed
from us by hundreds of years, it was very generally
supposed that Hebrew was the primeval language ;
and that the gods and stories of mythology were
either derived from the circumstances recorded in the
Old Testament, or else were events of general history
clothed by time in fables, more or less obscure and
distorted. The great scholars of the sixteenth and
seventeenth centuries, distinguished by their immense
erudition and untiring industry, have been of inestim-
able service in handing down to us the Classical
materials for research. As far as their lights
permitted, they, as of course, did more than justice
to Semitic influence in regions Hellenic ; and, after
all necessary abatements, such names as *e.g.*, that of
Bochart, will ever be held in honour. But they were
succeeded by an inferior race, marked by an ever
narrowing view, a portentous bigotry, and a philology
which, lasting in many instances well into the present
century, expired at length in a mere nightmare of
absurdities. Says Prof. Skeat :—

'I have had so much to unlearn, during the
endeavour to teach myself, owing to the extreme
folly and badness of much of the English etymo-

6

logical literature current in my earlier days, that the
avoidance of errors [by him] has been impossible;'
and he alludes to 'the playful days of Webster's
Dictionary . . . when the derivation of native
English words from Ethiopic and Coptic was a
common thing' (*Principles of Eng. Etymol.* 2nd
series, p. ix).

During the last 150 years England has also produced a curious race of 'Cranks,' by no means yet
extinct, who have brought forth various extraordinary works purporting to explain all the history,
mystery and belief of the past on philological and
general lines purely imaginary. Some of these pro-
ductions in their day took an honoured place in
almost every library; and, from their appearance in
booksellers' catalogues, would seem still to command
high prices, a touching illustration of the value which
mankind almost always puts upon certain peculiar
kinds of folly. I do not name any of them, as they
are quite unworthy even of such publicity as may be
afforded by the pillory.

The follies of Mr. Casaubon and his brethren
produced in the earlier part of this century a great
reaction, in which Germany took the lead. The old-
fashioned notions were contemptuously abolished
almost *en bloc*. The motto of this new school was
'Greece for the Greeks.' Numerous ancient errors
perished for ever, but, unfortunately, with them a
certain proportion of truth was also thrown overboard. Semitic influence in Greece was scouted as
an absurdity; and perhaps the high water mark in
this reaction was reached when 'Kadmos' was
declared to be a pure Hellenic name. That time has
gone by; and now the schoolboy can read in his

Liddell and Scott: 'Κάδμος. The man from the East ; cf. Hebr. *Kedem.*' Such is

> ' Action and reaction
> The miserable see-saw of our child-world.'

But the German Classical school were, despite their errors, immeasurably superior to the folly which they overthrew ; and such names as *e.g.*, Otfried Müller, will ever remain examples of a superb Classical scholarship, which erred in many details only because it was necessarily ignorant of a mass of knowledge, much of which is a commonplace even to the smatterer of to-day.

Upon this great scientific advance there followed, its cause being mainly due in the first instance to the British power in India, the gradual rise of a scientific comparative philology, bringing in its train the great truth of the original unity of the Aryan or Indo-European nations, and necessarily producing a study of comparative mythology, which in its logical development, is, as of course, not merely Aryan, but also Semitic, Turanian, and world-wide. The life of Prof. Max Müller, the leading exponent in England of this mighty movement, almost covers its present historical extent. Upon its discoveries and its merits I need not dwell. In this work I am concerned in the endeavour to show that the Aryanists, like the Classical phalanx of Otfried Müller, carried away by the splendour of their achievements, have pushed their claims too far, and have not conceded sufficient place to that great historical influence, which, as the years roll, it becomes ever clearer and clearer that the Semitic East exercised upon archaic Hellas. ' The gods will give us some faults to make us men.' The Churches 'of Jerusalem, Alexandria, and Antioch

6 *

have erred'; and shall the Assemblies of Mythologists altogether escape a similar fate ?

Contemporaneous with this last-named movement came that astonishing advance in our knowledge of the ancient and archaic non-Classical world, which we denote by such terms as Egyptology and Assyriology, the latter expression very incorrect indeed, but perhaps too well established in use and general understanding to be altered now. The buried past has risen majestic from the grave of ages, and her train of shadowy kings,—scoffed at by many a great Classical scholar such as Cornewall Lewis,—confronts us as living realities, and even in some instances, like that of a Ramesses the Great, actually face to face. Champollion, Lepsius, Birch, Mariette, Maspero, Renouf, Grotefend, Rawlinson, George Smith, what a debt we owe to them, and to their worthy followers and successors in these supremely interesting and important studies.

Lastly, Anthropology has taken the field, represented by many an acute and industrious student and compiler. All honour to them, and success to their efforts ! In dealing with the past, skilled assistance from every quarter is most valuable ; particularly as the problems to be attacked are almost invariably complex in character, being frequently partly explicable on one line of research and partly on another.

II. Certain difficulties of the Student in England

In England the student of the higher and obscurer branches of knowledge, unless he chance to be altogether exceptionally favoured by circumstance and environment, will probably find his lot rather a hard one. He must not expect any of that Government support which France and Germany so carefully and so admirably extend to rising talent. He must renounce all that popularity and the substantial rewards which are bestowed upon the abler of those artists whose themes are morbid piety, prudery, petticoats, or popular demonology. Nor must he expect much sympathy from his more fortunate brethren, until indeed he has become an important personage. Reviewers and critics, should they condescend to notice him, will probably treat him with but scant courtesy, especially if he chance not to reside in London, Oxford, or Cambridge. And if any well-disposed Nicodemus ventures faintly to ask for a patient hearing for the unfortunate wight, he will be contemptuously told that no profit of any kind arises out of Galilee. I am aware that the reviewer has been much found fault with of late (Vide *sup.* p. 32); and we must ever remember that his task is often a very hard one, and that the constant and necessary assumption of a diluted omniscience, whilst all the time he may be but too conscious of a very real and genuine ignorance, will frequently reveal a weary face when the mask is withdrawn. The student, moreover, may often find that unless by some means he can gain the goodwill of certain circles, coteries or cliques, let him write as he may, he will, to a considerable extent, be left out in the cold. I have known several painful instances where men of great powers and great knowledge have dropped sadly and prematurely into the grave, crushed by a grinding poverty and an unjust neglect. But it is not in the nature of the Englishman to yield in such a struggle. And just as our colossal and so deeply envied Empire has been almost entirely built up by the unaided, and even often deeply thwarted, efforts of private individuals, so in the grand fields of research the high-hearted student, even if this great authority be ignorant of him and that important centre acknowledge him not, will yet work on, whilst health and strength permit, content to try to do his duty, however unnoticed and obscure. And I can, from my own experience, assure him of this, that such studies, pursued for their own sake, grow sweeter even as they grow more arduous ; and that I for one am deeply grateful to Greeks, Etruscans, Babylonians and others, for the delightful problems which they have bequeathed to us.

III. General Standpoint of the Aryo-Semitic School

The Aryo-Semitic school of Hellenic mythologists, whilst fully recognizing the immense services rendered to the cause of knowledge by the old Classical scholars and the Aryanists, and also duly acknowledging the valuable assistance of anthropological research, endeavours, as the special feature of its method, to give the fullest effect to the ever-increasing mass of light which has been thrown by modern discovery upon the archaic history of Egypt and Western Asia in their relation to Hellas. They recognize that for hundreds of years before the commencement of the Olympiads, the Greeks were in close contact with the mixed peoples of Asia Minor, Aryan, and non-Aryan, with the Phoenicians ; and, to some extent, even with the Egyptians, who, as early as the Sixth Dynasty, called the Mediterranean ' the Great Circle of the Ujinivu,' Sem.

Yivânas (*i.e.*, Javanians) = Ionians. The Aryo-
Semitic school gives, which others · do not, their
legitimate weight to these historical facts. Painting
and sculpture, architecture, astronomy, and arithmetic
(Vide Strabo, XVI. ii. 24), the arts of commerce and
navigation, weights and measures, the treasures of the
forge and the loom, for such gifts as these, and ·for
many other features of civilization the Greek, as we
know, was indebted to the non-Aryan East. That
when he received them, he breathed upon them the
splendour and the energy of his own genius is
nothing to the present purpose. We know likewise
that in the well-known historical period the Greek,
like the Roman after him, was ever most willing to
receive the foreign divinity and to adopt the foreign
ritual. Adônis was the darling of the Athenian
matrons of the time of the Peloponnesian war;
Alexander accepted Melqârth and Amen, Yahveh and
Bel, as fast as he met with their ritual and their
votaries (Vide Hogarth, *Alexander of Macedon*, p. 209);
and, when Zeus-Jupiter had long been degraded to a
mere planetary genius, Isis, Serapis and Mithras
swayed the conservative religionists of the Roman
Empire. Apart from evidence, therefore, is it not
probable that the archaic Greek, a semi-barbarian
with an immense capacity for borrowing, would take
somewhat of the religion and ritual of those to whom
he owed so much in other ways, and who, from
the point of knowledge and civilization, were so
greatly his superiors? It would, moreover, be all
the easier for him to do this as, to a very great extent,
he could do it almost unconsciously. And the cause
of this lies in the fact that the Greek was ever prone
to find his own divinities in the gods of the nations

whom he met. Again and again he speaks of Zeus
and Hêra, Athêna and Artemis, when in reality
he refers to Semitic divinities entirely distinct.
Hêrodotos goes to Egypt, and finds there almost
all his Greek gods in full force ; just as men since
have talked about Juno at Carthage (Vide *sup.* p. 47).
And this constant habit of the Greek mind, utterly
misunderstood, has caused immense confusion in the
views and writings of mythologists.   Taking such
statements as true, *verbatim et literatim*, they have
indulged in a vast amount of absolute nonsense.
And, although now every scholar understands how
these presentments of fact by Hêrodotos and others
are to be received, yet, even at the present day, such
a giant in scholarship as Prof. Max Müller apparently
believes that *e.g.*, the goddess Athêna Onka of
Thebes is indeed a variant of his own beloved
Ahanâ.

Next, what is the philological aspect of the
question ? We do not compare the names of Roman
and Peruvian divinities because there is neither
a linguistic nor an historical connexion between
the two nations.   And if we find similar customs
among them, *e.g.*, each buried their erring vestal
virgins alive, we see that such usages spring from
causes which operate upon the general mind of
mankind, and are independent of any special
circumstances.   We compare the divinities of Vedic
India and of Greece, because there was once an
historical connexion between the ancestors of Indians
and Greeks; and because investigation shows that
their languages are in reality but variant dialects
of a common original.   Now suppose that these
two nations had spoken languages philologically

unconnected, but had long dwelt side by side; and
that India had bestowed upon Greece nearly all the
rudiments of civilization, including, as of course,
various words and names, it would have been
quite legitimate to investigate whether some Vedic
divinities might not, under these circumstances,
have found an entrance into the Hellenic Pantheon.
To give an instance of such a borrowing, and I take
it from Prof. Müller, although elsewhere he implies
that there are no such cases. Chaïtan (= Arabic
Shaitan, Heb. Satan) appears in the Mordvinian
Pantheon (Vide *C.* p. 250), and Christus in the
Wotjakian (*Ib.* pp. 465, 468). Thus, there may be,
and often has been, a borrowing of divinities between
nations who dwelt side by side, although their
languages have belonged to different families of
speech. Such a connexion may be called historical,
as opposed to linguistic. Who doubts the equation
—Persian Khshayârshâ = Gk. Xerxês? But its
truth does not depend upon the fact that Iranian and
Greek are two dialects of an original common speech.
Its basis is purely historical, viz., that at a certain
time the Greeks came in contact with a certain
King of Persia, and did their best (such as it was)
to reproduce his name in a Greek form. As all
scholars admit that the Sk. Dyaus = Gk. Zeus, so
are they equally clear that the Ph. Melqârth ('City-
King')= Gk. Melikertês (Vide *C.* p. 219) ; and this
latter equation may stand as the corresponding illustrative example in the Aryo-Semitic school. As the
one equation logically involves much besides itself
(Vide *sup.* p. 19), so also does the other. And
from the foregoing considerations it will at once
be evident that we violate no philological principle

when, with due care, we endeavour to explain certain
Greek names from Semitic sources.

IV. Semitic Indications in Greek Mythology

As the Greeks were an Aryan nation, the prior
probability is that a Greek divinity is an Aryan
divinity (Vide *sup.* p. 20). What, then, are the
indications of Semitic influence in particular
instances? The principal signs which point to the
Semitic origin of any particular personage of Hellenic
mythology are, (1) When neither his name, nor the
chief mythic incidents connected with his legend
appear in the other branches of Aryan religious-
mythology ; (2) When Aryan nature-myths do not
supply an easy and appropriate explanation of his
concept and history ; (3) When his cult is found in
regions either absolutely non-Aryan, or else permeated
with non-Aryan influence; (4) When his form is
more or less unanthropomorphic ; (5) When his
character and story generally are in harmony with
those of mythic personages admittedly non-Aryan ;
and (6) When the resources of Aryan philology are
powerless or inadequate to explain his name, and
some or many of his principal epithets.

It is to be remembered that the true and original
concept of a divinity is best arrived at by the correct
interpretation of his name, titles, and epithets; and
that almost every real explanation of the Hyponoia of
mythology is simple, and by its obvious suitability
to the case, justifies itself to an intelligent and
unprejudiced mind. Explanation of mythic incident,
or any etymon of a divinity-name which is utterly

strained and harsh, stands self-condemned.   And the
same is equally true of an attempted rendering of
a cuneiform tablet or of an Etruscan inscription.
When Dr. Deecke gave an utterly unnatural, forced,
quaint, and in itself improbable rendering of the
Etruscan inscription on the leaden plate of Magliano,
his effort stood self-condemned.   It hardly required
to be refuted by a jesting translation of the same
inscription by Prof. Pauli, which logically and
linguistically was in every way as good or better
than the serious attempt ; or the severe remark of
Prof. Bréal, ' Il y a quelque chose de plus extra-
ordinaire encore que cette traduction : c'est la
manière dont elle est justifiée.'

V.   'The Question of Allies'

Whilst I am alone responsible for many of the
applications to detail mentioned in this work, of the
general principles of the Aryo-Semitic school, on a
' question of Allies,' as Mr. Lang puts it, we may
claim the countenance and support of many great
names in the recent past and present.   An illustrious
adherent was the lamented François Lenormant,
whose death at the age of 47, was for the time an
almost irreparable loss.   It is impossible that the
torch of knowledge should, at all events at first, burn
with the same brightness in the hand of a disciple
who may have caught it as it fell from the dying
grasp of the master, as it did when firmly held on
high by the latter.   Many precious things are sacrificed at the funeral pyre of the illustrious dead.   But
alike in his Assyriological studies, and in such works
as *Les Premières Civilisations* (1874), *Les Origines
de L'Histoire* (1880-82), and the *Essai sur la Pro-*

pagation de L'Alphabet Phénicien, the master has left us a legacy of the highest value. Another example of sympathetic treatment is furnished by Maury in his well-known *Histoire des Religions de la Grèce Antique*. A crowd of scholars are rallying round the Aryo-Semitic banner, amongst whom I may mention such men as Prof. Max Duncker, author of the *History of Greece*; Canon Isaac Taylor, the well-known historian of the Alphabet ; and two other savants whose services to knowledge cannot easily be over valued, Prof. Sayce and Prof. Fritz Hommel. One of our latest and most powerful recruits is M. Victor Bérard, author of the *De l'Origine des Cultes Arcadiens* (1894). This accomplished writer, who combines an actual and practical knowledge of the locality of which he treats (always a great advantage), with keen acumen and an acquaintance with the latest authorities, bids fair, when his work is carefully weighed and its conclusions duly appreciated, to effect a revolution in many of the current ideas respecting a considerable portion of Greek mythology and legendary history. The vast erudition of Dr. Otto Gruppe, to whose special views on the origin of mythology I do not here refer, is also quite on our side.

There is another name which I can mention here with every respect and with a special pleasure, that of Sir Geo. W. Cox. It will ever remain his special achievement, by working on the analogical principle, to have crystalized into a harmonious whole the general application of the Natural Phenomena Theory to the details of Aryan mythology. The conclusions he has formulated have often been sneered at, seldom or never dealt with 'at grips,' as Mr. Lang would say.   In former works I have had at times to criticise his views, and to complain that his attitude respecting Semitic influence in Hellas was too much that of Prof. Max Müller.   Mr. Lang commences his Introduction to *M. M.* by observing that ' it may well be doubted whether works of controversy serve any useful purpose.'   Therefore, being before all things logical, he naturally proceeds to write a ' work of controversy ' ; and quotes a saying from Matthew Arnold, foolish, because untrue, that ' on an opponent one never does make any impression.'   Apropos of this baseless dogma, let me quote the following passage from the Preface to the second edition of Sir Geo. Cox's *Mythology of the Aryan Nations* (1881) :—

' During the twelve years which have passed since the publication of the first edition a large amount of solid work has been done within the domain of Comparative Mythology.   Of the results so gained probably the most important is the clearer light thrown on the influence of Semitic theology on the theology and religion of the Greeks.   This momentous question I have striven to treat impartially ; and for my treatment of it I have to acknowledge my obligations to Mr. Robert Brown's valuable researches in the field of the great Dionysiak Myth.'

I quote the above passage, not at all in my own honour, but simply in that of Sir Geo. Cox.   Had he modified his views under the influence of a great man, like Prof. Max Müller, or of a prominent and fashionable man like Mr. Andrew Lang, we might not perhaps have been surprised.   But that he, as a fact, did modify his conclusions on the matter, and thereby became, and is, in touch and harmony with the Aryo-Semitic school, simply from a careful consideration of the arguments urged by so humble a student as myself, shows an honesty of purpose and a devotion to truth of a very high order. Human nature is better than Matthew Arnold deemed it.

VI. An instance of the results of the Historical Method

Although our school is specially historical, and we often discover the true meaning of legendary narrative rather in the disputes and contests between hostile tribes and religionists on earth, than in ideas drawn from the successions and discords of the forces of nature, yet it must always be remembered that, as *e.g.*, Prof. Müller has most fully shown, the Natural Phenomena Theory is not merely of Aryan, but of world-wide application. A dawn-myth may be Phoenician, as well as Vedic (Cf. Gruppe, *Der phoinikische Urtext der Kassiepeïalegende*, 1888). But there is one recent instance in which the successful application of the historical method, has so signally put to flight a whole mass of supposed impalpable myth, idle legend and mere invention, an instance so important and so far reaching in its logical consequences, that I cannot leave it here unmentioned. I refer to the complete and most remarkable demonstration of the historical accuracy of the writer of the xivth chapter of the Book of *Genesis*. Times innumerable have the campaign of Kudur-Lagamar (Chedorlaomer) in the West, his overthrow by Abraham, and the story of Melchizedek been treated as an Oriental romance, incredible, impossible, as baseless as the tale of Judith and Holofernes. Or, again, it has been explained as an elaborate piece of

astronomical symbolism, veiling high and wondrous
truths. But, thanks to such quiet, patient workers
as my friend Mr. T. G. Pinches of the British Museum,
to the labours of Prof. Sayce, and above all, in this
instance, to the brilliant results achieved by Prof.
Hommel (*The Ancient Hebrew Tradition as illustrated
by the Monuments*, Eng. Edit. 1897), the secrets of
history, faithfully preserved by the imperishable
cuneiform tablets, stand revealed. Now there pass
before us the great form of the Elamite conqueror;
the mighty Khammurabi-Amraphel, true founder of
the grandeur of Babylon; the majestic figure of the
Priest-king of Uru-salim ('the-City-of-Peace'); and,
lastly, as a necessary corollary, we see in Abraham
no eponymous tribal hero, no imaginary personifica-
tion of the Nocturnal-heaven, but a noble form of
flesh and blood consisting, a mighty Shaykh, the
terror of the oppressor and the marauder, and the
follower, and therefore the friend, of the eternal
God.

I do not hesitate to say that the result of the
splendid discoveries which have now been made by
such men as Hommel, Glaser, Sayce and others, not
merely reveals to us the amazingly important part
played by archaic Arabia in the history and development of religion, and throws a flood of light upon
many a dark and difficult passage in the Old Testament. It does all this indeed, but far more also. It
shakes to the foundation the whole vast recent theory
and system of the comparatively late origin and
composition of the earlier books of the Bible; that
huge house of cards reared mainly by Wellhausen
with infinite skill and pains, and which, really based
chiefly upon nescience and what was for the time

being apparent probability, and so eagerly daubed
by disciples in Germany and in England with much
untempered mortar, now totters to its fall. And
these results affect not merely our views about the
Hexateuch. The whole critical system of the school
of Wellhausen stands discredited. Men may attempt
to show that such and such a *Psalm* was written in
honour of one of the Ptolemies ; or, if they like, that
the *Song of Songs* was specially composed for Antony
and Kleopatra. But the heart has gone out of the
business. Khammurabi has dealt the system of
Wellhausen its death blow.

VII. The Contests of the Gods and Heroes

The contests of the gods and heroes related in
myth and archaic legend are based, wholly or mainly,
upon one or more of the three following circumstances :—(1) The apparent succession and conflict
of the ordinary phenomena of nature ; (2) The
actual contests and oppositions of the rival votaries of
clashing faiths and cults ; and (3) The fancies of
archaic poets and mythographers, these being not
wholly arbitrary, but shaped and moulded more or
less in accordance with an almost infinite number of
pre-existing facts, myths, and floating beliefs.

The Natural Phenomena Theory has made us
familiar with an immense number of instances in
Aryan mythology of contests based upon the first of
these three causes. But it applies in almost equal
force elsewhere. Witness in Egypt the contests
between Asar (Osiris, probably derived from the
Akkadian Marduk-Asari), Râ, and Har (Horus) on
the one side ; and Set and the monster Tebha
(Typhon) on the other. Or witness the Euphratean

story of a contest between the Sun-god and the Moon-god (often the Diad of hostile brethren), which centuries after amongst the Persians, took an Euhemeristic character as the rivalry between two opposing satraps Nannaros (Ak. Nannar, a name of the Moon-god) and Parsondês (Vide Sayce, *Rel. Anct. Babs.* p. 157 *et seq.*). The *Iliad* furnishes us with the most famous instances of contests of divinities arising from the third of these causes.

But it is with the second of these three underlying sets of circumstances, that the Aryo-Semitic student of Greek mythology is specially concerned. No view of natural phenomena will adequately explain them. No mere poetic fancy called them into being. To take an instance. A well-known, but reverently-regarded, legend told how Hêraklês held a mysterious contest with Apollôn for the possession of the Delphic Tripod; and how the strife between these two mighty personages was only terminated by the direct intervention of Zeus, who severed them by a flash of lightning (For a good Vase-illustration of this scene, vide Walters, *Cat. of the Gk. and Et. Vases in the Brit. Mus.* Vol. ii (1893), p. 22. As Hêraklês is moving off with the Tripod, Apollôn following, seizes one of its legs; Artemis stands behind him, Athêna behind Hêraklês). Here the Natural Phenomena Theory is powerless to aid us. We can understand indeed by its assistance how the solar hero Hêraklês can borrow the golden boat-cup of Hêlios, to enable him to sail over the western ocean. For here Hêlios stands confessed as the Sun, pure and simple; and the mythic phrases which tell of the solar hero and the solar barque blend harmoniously. But a personal strife of a great (Aryan) Sun-god against a great

7

(Aryan) Sun-god, and especially against so truly
national and revered a figure as Apollôn, who, with
Athêna, perhaps best represents the splendour of
Hellas at the brief moment of her culmination, is
almost inconceivable. No poet or mythographer
would ever have dared to excogitate such an idea.
Like Hêrodotos, they were all far too *god-fearing*.
We know, moreover, from various sources and indications that Delphoi was a great centre of rival, and, at
times, contending, cults ; and this circumstance it is,
which constitutes the true Hyponoia of the legend.
Mr. Farnell, with whom I am often happy to find
myself in agreement, well remarks :—

' No doubt there were physical reasons why Helios
and why Poseidon should be worshipped at Corinth;
but the Corinthian legend of this strife, the Delphic
legend of the contest . . of Apollo and Heracles for
the tripod, the Attic legend of the rivalry of Poseidon
and Athena, and many other similar theomachies,
probably all contain the same kernel of historical
fact, an actual conflict of worships—an earlier
cherished by the aboriginal men of the locality, and a
later introduced by the new settlers' (*Cults*, i. 270).

VIII. Hêraklês

Hêraklês is not found in the mythology of the
other branches of the Aryan nations, and his name,
for all its intensely Greek appearance, the Aryanistic
philologist is unable to explain (Vide *C.* pp. 612, 632).
I am not concerned here to deny that there may
perhaps have been a native Hellenic god so called ;
but it is quite certain that, if such there were, he
disappears, like a double star, in the overlapping

splendour of his great brother, the Semitic toiling,
warring, voyaging, travelling, man-slaying, at times
maniacal, Sun-god ; whose end is naturally, as Prof.
Müller expresses it, 'the sun's death in the fiery
clouds.' Prof. Müller excellently illustrates, on the
lines of the Natural Phenomena Theory, many
incidents in the Hêraklês-myth ; but all such illustrations are quite as applicable to a Semitic, as to an
Aryan, Sun-god. And, as will be seen (Vide *inf.*
p. 194) it is just in connexion with some of these
exploits of Hêraklês upon which the Aryan mythologist has little or nothing to say, that the Semitic
connexion of the hero throws the clearest and most
remarkable light. I am quite aware of the ordinary
view, one, *e.g.*, usually found in English Diction-
aries of Mythology, that the doings of a Semitic
Sun-god of the Outer-world were, in comparatively
late times, arbitrarily tacked on to a native Hellenic
Sun-god of the Inner-world. But this theory
altogether collapses under careful examination conducted by the light of modern discoveries. Hêraklês,
the dweller at Thebes and at Tiryns ; the opponent
of such purely Aryan divinities as Hêra, Aïdês
(Vide *inf.* p. 196), Apollôn, and Arês ; the Lion-
slayer (Vide R. B. Jr., *Eridanus*, Appendix iii. The
Sun-god and the Lion), first worshipped in Greece at
the Phoenician Mârath (Marathôn ; cf. Paus. I.
xxxii. 4) ; linked by a thousand ties and incidents
with Western Asia, and especially with Phoenicia
and her colonies, is in all probability Phoenician in
name as in nature—Harekhal ('*the* Traveller.' Vide
inf. p. 195 ; Bérard, *Cultes Arcad.* p. 257). As Prof.
Duncker well sums up the matter :—

    'Marathon bears the same name as Marathus
                                        7 *

(Amrit) in Crete, and on the Phoenician coast near Aradus; a fountain springing at Marathon is called Macaria, "in honour of Heracles"; *i.e.*, it bears the name of Melkarth, which the Greeks modified into Melicertes and Makar; the district of Marathon worshipped Heracles ; indeed, it boasted that it had been the first of all the Hellenic countries to worship him.   Heracles is Archal, the labouring, striving, fighting Baal Melkarth of the Phoenicians' (*Hist. of Greece*, i. 62-3).

And, here, let me remark in passing, that we often meet with much really baseless assertion respecting the alleged comparatively modern date of this or that Greek myth ; the reason given generally being that it is not mentioned by earlier writers.   As, however, some three-fourths of early Greek literature has perished, such reasons and opinions are generally of very slender value.   Moreover, as a rule, the argument from silence must be regarded with very grave suspicion.   The altogether undue weight too frequently attributed to it, has again and again led writers into opinions really untenable, and often actually ridiculous.

IX.   Athêna v. Poseidôn

Few stories are more familiar than that of the great Attic contest between Athêna and Poseidôn for supremacy at Athênai, a city the plural form of whose name probably indicates, according to the acute suggestion of Prof. Sayce, that, like various other Greek towns, it was originally the scene of a combination of distinct tribes or nationalities, each dwelling in its own quarter ; as is the case at present in various Oriental cities.   We know how in the merit-competition Athêna produced the olive and Poseidôn the war-horse, the Ak. *ansu-kurra* ('animal from the East'), between which, also appearing as the Sea-horse, and the god there is ever the closest connexion; and from which he is styled Hipparchos, Hippêgetês, Hippios, Hippodromios, Hippomedôn, etc. This is no contest between the Dawn and the Sea, and no mere idle invention. It is a true, though veiled, relation of a time when the destiny of Athens trembled in the balance, a remote epoch when King Porphyriôn ('the Purple-man,' *i.e.*, the Phoenician) reigned there and worshipped his Aphrodîtê Ourania (Vide Paus. I. xiv. 7), who as Mr. Farnell, amongst others, has shown with great learning and ability (Vide *Cults*, ii. 658 *et seq*.), in origin was no goddess of high and holy passion as opposed to Aphrodîtê Pandêmos, but simply the Oriental love-goddess 'Aschthârth (Astartê). Ourania is but the translation of her title Melekhet-Haschâmaîm ('Queen-of-heaven'). Had Poseidôn, the representative of the Phoenician element, prevailed; had Athens become another Carthage, the destinies of the world might indeed have flowed in a different channel. But the same genius which rolled back the tide of barbarism at Marathôn and Salamis, equally prevailed on this momentous occasion; and Erichthonios ('the Man-of-the-earth') also an epithet of Poseidôn himself (Vide Hêsych. in voc. *Erechtheus*), and with good reason,—the child of Gê, connected with the Serpent, which to the Hellenes is a symbol of the earth, Erichthonios, otherwise Erechtheus, representative of the native Attic race, stretched forth his baby arms to the divine Athêna-Ahanâ, who took him once and for ever to her breast. The peculiar epithet

Kynadês (' Dog-faced,'= ἀνελεύθερος, ' treacherous '—
of animals) applied to Poseidôn by the Athenians,
appears to have some connexion with this great
event. The scene is well represented on a Cornetan
vase (Figured in Roscher, *Lex.* p. 1305). Gê, a
female figure, partly concealed by the ground, holds
up the little naked Erichthonios, who stretches out
his arms to Athenaia ; whilst the goddess, stooping
slightly, with sweet and gracious dignity, holds out
her hands to receive him. Behind her, staff in hand,
stands the naked figure of Hêphaistos, representative
of the craftsman's art in that aspect in which it is
associated with masculine toil and effort, and who,
combined with Athêna, completes the art-circle.
Behind Gê is Poseidôn (on whom the boy turns his
back) in true Dagonic form, a demi-man of noble
aspect, but from the waist downwards a sea-monster
in huge spiral curls.

The female ' reflection ' of this Sea-god is the
Sea-goddess whom we meet in many places. Thus,
she appears on Babylonian seals ; or, again, as
Atar-'Ati (Atargatis-Derketô) of Ashqelôn. Pausanias (VIII. xli. 4) encountered her near Phigaleia,
represented as a statue, woman to the waist and fish
below. The antiquaries of the place called her
Eurynomê (Vide *inf.* p. 117), whilst people generally
regarded her as Artemis. Pausanias very justly
observes, that he cannot understand what possible
connexion can exist between Artemis and a figure of
this kind. She was also called Artemis Limnâtis
(Paus. IV. iv. 2) or Limnaia (*Ib.* II. vii. 6), ' the
Lady of the Lake.' Lucian, or whoever else may
have written the monograph *On the Syrian Goddess*,
met with her in Phoenicia. He says, ' I saw a statue

of Derketô in Phoenicia, and a strange sight it is, half
woman, while the half from thigh to toe extends as
the tail of a fish ' (Sec. xiv). Troizên, in Argolis,
affords another excellent instance of the wide-spread
and prolonged contest between Athêna and Poseidôn,
which here ended in a drawn battle followed by
peace. Says Pausanias (II. xxx. 6) :—

' The Troizênians reverence their country, if any
people do. And they say that Ôros [= Tzur-os,
i.e., Tyre. Cf. ' Ζωρός, quem conditorem Carthaginis
facit Appian ' Gesen. *Script. Ling. Ph.* p. 415. So
the Babylonian god-name Uras reappears in ' the
Assyrian king ' Horus of Pliny, *Hist. Nat.* xxx. 51 ;
vide Sayce, *Rel. Anct. Babs.* p. 152] lived first in their
land,' which was called Ôraia after him. This statement naturally rather perplexed good Pausanias, who
remarks that Ôros seems to him to be an Egyptian,
not a Hellenic, name. He continues the mythic
pedigree :—Lêïs (= Sem. Laish), daughter of Ôros
(Cf. *Judges*, xviii. 7, where Laish, as a locality, is a
daughter of Phoenicia), became by Poseidôn the
mother of Althêpos (' the Healer,'= Asklêpios). This
genealogy affords an interesting instance of how
such pedigrees were at times composed. Here, the
invading city is personified as the first dweller in the
country. Next, a place-name connected with her
is married to one of her divinities, the offspring of
the union being another of her divinities. It is thus
that we must deal with much of the mythic history
and genealogies preserved by Pausanias. Rightly
understood they contain a very valuable residuum of
archaic Hellenic records, such as we find scarcely
anywhere else. Mr. Gladstone once observed to me
that he valued Pausanias almost next after Homer ;

and indeed it is difficult to overestimate the importance of the *Periêgêsis*.

During the reign of Althêpos, one of those disputes
between Hellene and Phoenician, so many of which
are recorded by Pausanias, arose. The mythic form
is carefully preserved, so we read :—' They say that
Athêna and Poseidôn had a wrangle about the
country, and determined to hold it in common, for
thus Zeus ordered them to do. And on this account
they [the Troizênians] reverence Athêna naming her
Polias [' City-goddess,' a title the female equivalent
of Melqârth.] and Sthenias [' the Strong ']; and
Poseidôn they name "the King,"' *i.e.*, Melekh (Cf. the
Ammonite gods Môlekh and Milkom, 1 *Kings*, xi. 5, 7;
Zeus Meilichios, understood euphemistically as ' the
Kindly '). Thus, the mixed population of Troizên,
after the Phoenician fashion, resolved Poseidôn and
Athêna into a divine Diad, Melekh and Melekhet-
qârtha (=Gk. Astyanassa), the ' King ' and the
' Queen-of-the-city.' ' And thus their ancient coins
bear as a device a Trident and a head of Athêna.'
This last statement is perfectly correct, except that
Athêna is put first. Vide Percy Gardner, *Brit.
Mus. Cat. Gk. Coins, Peloponnesus* (1887), p. 165 :
· Troezen. *Before* B.C. 431 ; Ob. Female head, facing,
with long hair (Athene). Rev. Trident.' The
testimony of coins is frequently of immense value to
the mythologist.

Lastly, the poet takes up the story, and recounts
in deathless verse the long struggle between Uncle
and Niece over the person and fortunes of a
protagonistic Greek hero. Here, too, we see Athêna
at the last victorious; but, at the same time,
Poseidôn, although he may come off but second best

in the contest, is honoured and reverenced even
when seemingly defeated. We know this poem as
the *Odyssey*. And those who wish to apprehend the
true significance of the position of the Homeric
Poseidôn, compelled to bow to the will of Zeus in
the Inner World, but almost supreme in the Outer
World, cannot do better than avail themselves of the
subtle insight and almost matchless knowledge of
Homeric detail, and of its force and meaning, which
we find in the analysis of the god by Mr. Gladstone.

X. A Digression

As a modern youth, who, just entering into society
and the grand possibilities of public life, is fortunate
enough to secure for friend and patroness some
clever, powerful, influential, keen, yet tender-hearted,
woman of the world, of noble rank, a dozen years or
so older than himself, and who may perchance have
known and loved his mother,—such somewhat, if
I may illustrate great things by small, was the
position of the Athenian of the grand epoch which
ended about B.C. 440. How well has many a man
of the Victorian age progressed by the aid of such
a firm, wise guidance ; benefitted by an exquisite
tact, which has preserved him from follies, regulated
and directed his just ambitions, showed him how
to correct and conquer his deficiencies, how to make
his strong points still stronger, and to do full justice
to himself. She has led the coy goddess Opportunity
to his side, and made her kiss him. She has, it may
be, almost imperceptibly guided him to the choice
of a partner sweet and suitable ; and when, it may

be on his marriage morning, as he stoops before her, and she, as she imprints a kiss upon his brow, whispers, 'God bless you, my Child, your dear mother would indeed be proud if she could see you now,' with what feelings does an ardent, true and generous-hearted youth regard such a patroness? Although she be neither mother, sister, sweetheart, wife, does he not look upon her with a combined love and reverence so deep that he cannot fathom it, so tender and so sacred that it blends with the holiness of devotion. It is often asked, How did the Greeks regard their gods? I answer that a true-hearted Athenian of the great period looked thus upon Athêna, save only that her superhuman power and splendour vastly intensified his awe and his belief. And how was it that this noble and stimulating concept of divinity faded so early from the spirit of the City of the Violet Crown? Mainly, because it was materialized. After the mighty effort of the Persian War wealth and power fast flowed in upon the votaries of Athêna. As art advanced with an astonishing rapidity, the earlier representations of the goddess were felt to be not merely insufficient but ridiculous ; just as the archaic shrine, despite the hoary reverence which hung about it, became in measure contemptible. An Iktînos arose to build her a house, a Pheidias to crystalize into tangibility with matchless skill her ideal beauty, and her unseen yet finely apprehended strength. And then, O sad result of human powers at their highest, O cruel instance of the trail of blight which human genius is wont to cast behind it, Athêna enshrined in un-exampled splendour, vanished from the mind of her Athenians, as the Dawn pales in sunrise, save

that Pallas passed once and for ever. The City,
Athens, Akropolis, Parthenon, the Statues, they
became the goddess. Athêna fell from heaven to
earth, never to rise again. And when the sway of
Periklês, so brilliant yet so baneful, was over, he
could leave no successor; and, at his melancholy
close, had to hand on to frantic demagogues,
incapable dullards, and reckless aristocrats, devoid
even of the last rags of principle and of decency,
the city which he had glorified and the power which
he had centered in his single grasp. How such
successors in the course of a few years destroyed
the Athenian Empire, is one of the chief marvels
and pities of all time. And by the stern fate dealt
out to such a worthy, pious soul as Nikias, we learn
the truth that when the good man, through weakness
and despicable fear of his fellows, betrays those
principles of conduct and of action which his heaven-
guided soul warns him are true and noble, he must,
in just requital, drink the cup of punishment to the
last drop. The Republic rose, indeed, from her fall,
but with her once strong right arm withered, and her
head grey, as by the transit of long centuries of
weary effort. Her art had culminated, and therefore
now could be but imitative and decadent. Poetry
lay buried in the grave of Sophoklês. Her truest
sage and teacher she had persecuted and slain. Yet
one thing remained to her—the tongue. And in the
persons of Platôn and Demosthenês she bestowed
upon the world two such talkers as it had never
seen. The first of these, however little able either to
influence the times he lived in or his successors, was
yet honoured in his life and happy in his death,
passing from the stage whilst still the home of

Athêna and Erechtheus preserved its freedom. The second, less fortunate, lived to share in the rout from that fatal spot which the Greek of to-day calls Chĕrónĕa, and to suck the poison of the reed in the sanctuary of Poseidôn. The great talkers were, as of course, followed by smaller talkers, and they in turn by less; until we reach the epoch of the dwarfs of babble and gossip. One historian flashes a ray of brilliant light upon these pigmies. They had encountered a little man, but a great gentleman, 'a god-born soul true to its origin.' They had exclaimed, 'What does this Gutter-snipe (σπερμολόγος) want to say?' and half in idle curiosity, half in mere jest, they hurried him along to the Hill of Imprecations, and, probably placing him on the white stone of Impudence (Vide Paus. I. xxviii. 5),—for this would be part of the joke,—made a ring round him, and listened to an address which, from the fragment of it that has come down to us, must have been one of the finest and most skilful commendations of a cause which ever fell on ear. It had but small effect, and, as the years rolled on, the idle tongues still wagged, the philosophy got ever drier and more pithless, until its last professors fled from the rigour of Justinian, true type of cold-hearted persecuting bigotry, to seek for freedom at the hands of the barbarous despotism of Persia. Centuries passed ; the city of Kimôn and Themistoklês was enslaved and trampled upon, but the temple of Iktînos, unharmed by the gentle hand of pitying Time, still reared its matchless symmetry. It remained for the madness of Venetian and Turk, late in modern times, to shatter the sanctuary of the Virgin into utter ruin, and to leave it as it meets the eye to-day. Our own century has brought fresh chances. Greece has been in part delivered from the iron thraldom of the changeless barbarian of Central Asia. But she has done little for herself except talk. The melancholy events of the present raise ' for Greeks a blush, for Greece a tear.' If a Greek cannot fight bravely in the neighbourhood of Thermopylai, he must indeed be a poor creature. The Concert of Europe, whatever else it may have failed in, has at least prevented the step of the Turk from being again placed on the hill of the Akropolis; but, excepting Jerusalem, mother of sorrows, and matchless in her degradation, few, if any, of earth's famous cities have endured a humiliation so long and dreary, as has befallen the nobly-placed dwelling of Erechtheus, whence the light, touching the spear of the colossal Athêna, was wont to flash towards Sunium in the brief summer of the Hellenic world.

> ' Bear with me ;
> My heart is in the coffin there with Caesar,
> And I must pause till it come back to me.'

XI. Prof. Müller and M. Bérard

Having now, to some extent, set forth the principles of the Aryo-Semitic school, and illustrated them by a few examples, I will next consider in detail Prof. Müller's treatment of some of the principal figures in the Hellenic Pantheon for which we claim a Semitic origin. I first notice a reference which he makes to the work of M. Bérard (Vide *sup.* p. 92). He remarks that certain scholars, who entertain grave doubts respecting the identity of various

Greek and Vedic divinity-names, ' are satisfied with the vaguest similarities when they compare Semitic and Aryan names, without even attempting anything like a scientific etymological analysis' (*C.* p. 216). It will be observed that he speaks as if Greek were a language connected with the Semitic dialects, and as if the Semitist was bound to show a ' root'-connexion between this or that Greek and Semitic word or name. He does not, of course, mean this. Where connexion exists, it is one based on borrowing and transliteration, not on variant phases of an original unity. And our view of this connexion will depend in each case upon the degree of similarity, coupled with the history and general concept of the mythic personage. Nothing more, from the nature of the case, can be asked of us.

Miscalling the French writer ' Barard,' Prof. Müller devotes a single page to the 368 pages of his closely-reasoned and very learned treatise.' He mentions certain suggested Greek and Semitic equations, but only to dismiss them with the remark :—

' It is impossible to refute such assertions, because there is really no evidence to lay hold of and to examine.'

One of these suggestions is that the forms Êrigonê, Erykinê, etc., are at times, transliterations of the Semitic *Erek-hayîm* (not of a form ' Erek Hagim,' as Prof. Müller puts it), a title of Astartê translated by *Longae vitae auctor*. In support of this view, M. Bérard advances a whole body of evidence, with which it is clearly far too troublesome for Prof. Müller to deal in detail. He contents

himself with merely asserting that 'there is really no
evidence to examine,' and passes on.   Now it is,
of course, highly natural that Prof. Müller, after a
half a century of effort in a certain field, crowned
with brilliant success, should be utterly disinclined
to examine carefully a rival theory resting upon
numerous points of detail, and involving a delicate
weighing of evidence.   But such an attitude does
not dispose of the opposing evidence, which
remains as weighty as before.   After this, one is
almost surprised that he admits the equation
Melqârth = Melikertês.   But Prof. Müller certainly
takes just exception to a suggestion of M. Bérard,
which, however, is apparently made half jestingly,
' Presque tout l'Olympe grec est peut-être d'origine
sémitique' (p. 364).   If this be really meant
seriously, I am as much opposed to it as Prof. Müller
himself (Vide *sup.* p. 20).

XII. Prof. Müller on the Kabeiroi

I venture to assert, without any fear of contradiction from scholars generally, that the equation
Sem. Kabîrîm (' Great-ones ') = Gk. Kabeiroi, is as
firmly established as the equation Dyaus = Zeus.
This fact Prof. Müller does not venture to deny
either directly, or indirectly by suggesting an Aryan
etymon, but says :—

'The origin of the Kabeiroi seems to me so
mysterious and uncertain that I can derive no help
from them in deciphering the adventures of the
Dioskouroi.'   As the latter are Aryan personages

entirely distinct from the Kabîrîm, no such help
could ever be reasonably expected. He continues:—

'Their name [Kabeiroi] has been derived [He
means that attempts have been made to derive their
name] from every possible and impossible language.
. . I shall not add a new etymology, nor any
hypothesis about their origin' (*C.* p. 639). We may
feel quite certain that if he could have ventured to
claim them as Aryan gods, he would have done
so. He does not venture upon this, and so remains
mute about them ; and I cannot but regard the
instance as showing very forcibly how utterly
disinclined he is to admit even the most familiar
cases of Semitic influence in Hellas, if, in any way,
it is possible to avoid expressly making the
admission. The Kabeiric cult was naturally in full
force in Boiôtia, where the Epigonoi are stated to
have put a stop to it for a time. The Kabeiroi were
said to have taken signal vengeance on Persian
and Macedonian profaners of their shrine (Paus. IX.
xxv. 6, 7).

XIII. Kronos

Kronos, like Poseidôn, Dionysos, Aphrodîtê and
Hêraklês, does not appear in any form or phase
either in the Vedic Hymns, or in the religion and
mythology of any Aryan nation except the Greeks.
Readers of Prof. Müller and Mr. Lang are aware
what a puzzle this strange figure is to them.
Mr. Lang, who calls him ' Cronos,' a form neither

Greek nor Latin, gets quite crusty over him, styles him 'an odious ruffian,' and declares, with some triumph : —

'Now, I have offered no explanation at all of who Cronos was, what he was god of, from what race he was borrowed, from what language his name was derived. The fact is that I do not know' (*M. M.* p. 36).

We quite believe him ; but the air with which he makes his declaration of nescience, irresistibly reminds one of a remark in Miss Edgeworth's *Frank*, 'If you are thankful for your ignorance, you have doubtless a great deal to be thankful for.'

The first point for consideration in any investigation about such a personage as Kronos, is, Where do we primarily chiefly meet with him ? The answer is, In the works of a Boiôtian poet, Hêsiod, whose family had settled in Aiolis. The whole archaic history of Boiôtia shows it to have been a special centre of Semitic influence. Even Prof. Müller observes :—

'It has been a very generally received opinion that in the names of Kadmos as well as of some of his descendants we have indications of Phenician immigration, and that his name and that of his grandson Melikertes suffice to prove this. This may be so' (*C.* p. 647).

As in the case of the Kabeiroi, he declines to admit what almost every other school regards as nearly a truism. But when we turn to the Semitic side, to the Phoenician kosmogony and to the

mythologico-religious fragments of early Phoenician
belief which have been preserved by Philôn of
Byblos under the name of the writings of
Sanchouniathôn, we meet with Kronos again, and
acting in his usual apparently extraordinary manner.
If anyone should suggest that these fragments are
comparatively modern forgeries, I answer that the
labours of Movers, Bunsen, Lenormant, and others
have proved such an opinion to be not only
untenable, but ridiculous. Whether there ever was
an actual Phoenician sage called Sanchouniathôn, or
whether, as the witty American said of Homer, 'his
works were written by another fellow of the same
name,' is altogether immaterial. A Greek philosopher
of the age of Philôn could no more have forged these
fragments than Damaskios, the last of the Neo-
Platonists, could have concocted the archaic
Euphratean kosmogony which he has so well
preserved, or than an Assyriologist of to-day could
have invented the correspondence contained in the
Tablets of Tel-el-Amarna.

As Prof. Müller and Mr. Lang have showed at
length, the myths of various races speak of the
primeval embrace of Heaven and Earth. They lay
together in the darkness, and their severance, when
it came, must have been effected by light. Kronos,
therefore, at this stage of the story, is necessarily
a Light-power. As anthropomorphic analogies are
rigidly maintained, this severance is accompanied by
a mutilation which is a logical sequence of the
anthropomorphic mould in which the story is cast.

Here is the point in the tale at which to enquire
into the etymon of the name 'Kronos.' Prof. Tiele, a
most weighty authority, observes :—

'Mr. Lang has justly rejected the opinion of Welcker and Mr. Max Müller, that Cronos is simply formed from Zeus's epithet, Κρονίων' (Ap. M. M. p. 31).

Prof. Müller says :—

'Κρόνος, may [Italics mine.], whatever may be said to the contrary, stand dialectically for χρόνος, time' (C. p. 507).

This is merely a child of despair. If Prof. Müller were arguing against this view, with what force and copiousness of illustration would he insist that a name of this abstract meaning never was and never could be bestowed upon a primitive Aryan divinity; that these gods always embody some physical idea, such as the bright sky, dawn, sun opening the gate of the morning, etc. Twenty years ago, in The Great Dionysiak Myth, as Mr. Lang notes (M. M. p. 35), I explained Kronos as = Karnos ('Horned'). Let us examine this view. An objection subsequently made by Mr. Lang that Kronos is not represented as wearing horns, is natural enough ; but, as we shall see, really not to the point. The Assyrio-Babylonian word qarnu, 'horn,' reappears in Hebrew and Phoenician as qeren. In Semitic usage, 'horn' (as e.g., often appears in the Old Testament) is used as the equivalent of 'power,' the 'Horned-one' = the 'Powerful-one.' Thus, we read in Sanchouniathôn (i. 7) that 'Aschthârth (= Astartê), the Bab. Ishtar or Istar, 'She-Baal the Cow' (LXX in Tobit, i. 5) 'put a bull's head upon her head, as the mark of her sovereignty.' She is the Axiokersê of the Samothracian mysteries, as

8 *

Dionysos is the Axiokersos (Vide *inf.* p. 143) and
we meet her elsewhere as Ashtoreth Qarnâim
(' Astartê-of-the-Two-horns,' *Gen.* xiv. 5). Similarly,
Philôn, who of course regarded Kronos as an Hellenic
divinity, which indeed he became, always renders
the name of the Semitic god Îl or Êl (' the Powerful ') by ' Kronos,' in which usage we have a lingering
feeling of the real meaning of the name. Now from
Q-e-R-e-N naturally arises such a form as K-e-R-e-
N-os, Karnos. But, in such cases the Greek was
often wont to drop the first vowel. Thus, the Sem.
Kar-kôm = Gk. Κρό-κος. Karnos, therefore, naturally,
reappears as ' Kronos ' (' the Powerful '). *Qarnâim*,
as the name of a horned divinity, reappears in the
name and cult of the rayed (= horned) Sun-god
Apollôn Karnaios, so ancient and famous amongst
the Dorians; and which, as Otfried Müller has
showed, ' was derived from Thebes ' (*Doric Race*,
i. 373). One idle story said that this worship was
established by an imaginary Karnos, an Akarna-
nian. Another told that Apollôn was called Karnaios
from some connexion with his cornel trees (κρανείας)
which had been profanely cut down; and that the
Greeks, having propitiated him, called him Karnaios,
' transposing the ρῶ according to ancient custom '
(Paus. III. xiii. 3). This passage clearly shows that
there was an ancient transposition of the ρ of some
kind or another. And the Semitic connexion of
Karnaios well appears in the statement of Praxilla,
quoted by Pausanius, that he was the son of Εurôpê
(*i e.*, *Erebh*, ' the West,' as the side of sunset and
darkness, whence is derived the Gk. Ἔρεβος, primarily
' the Gloom-after-sunset '), the sister of Kadmos.

Kronos, of whom Karnaios is a variant, also reappears as the radiant and glorious Sun-god in the familiar and beautiful passage in Pindar (*Olymp.* ii) where is described the happiness of those blessed heroes who ' accomplish their way on the path of Zeus to the tower [*i.e.*, secure-abode, like παράδεισος, from Old Pers. *pairidaêza,* = peri-dyke.] of Kronos.' There Kronos, assisted in his sway by Rhadamanthys (= Eg. Rhot-amenti, ' King-of-the-West '; or Under-world), has the highest throne; there, too, dwell Pêleus (According to M. Bérard, = πηλός, Lat. *lutum* = Sem. *thîth*, Thetis) and Kadmos.

But, perhaps the reader may say, yes, yes, all very well, ' almost thou persuadest me.' Yet, surely, was not Kronos a Darkness-power? Did he not swallow nearly everybody he could lay hands on? not in cannibal fashion, as some wiseacres have suggested, for he brought them all up again none the worse; but like the Egyptian ' Crocodile of the West which fed upon the setting stars ' (Renouf. *Rel. Anct. Egypt,* p. 108), or the monster down in the sea, which, having swallowed the sun, ' spat out its prey again on the shore ' (Goldziher, *Mythol. among the Hebs.* p. 101) next morning. Does not Homer tell us that Zeus has imprisoned Kronos and the Titans beneath earth and sea? Yea, verily, but have patience. Let us hasten slowly.

In the Phoenician kosmogony preserved by Pherekŷdês of Syros, the instructor of Pythagoras, and a few fragments of which have come down to us, it is stated that at first the world was ruled by Ophîon, Γέρων 'Οφίων (= Sem. *Nâkhâsh qadmûn*), and Eurynomê (= Sem. *Erebhno'emâ,* ' Beautiful-night.' The independent Gk. name Eurynomê is here applied by way of transliteration), who were hurled from

heaven and power by Kronos (Îl) and Rhea (Ammâ).
In Homer Eurynomê (= Artemis Limnâtis, etc.
Vide *sup.* p. 102) has become a daughter of Ocean
(*Il.* xviii. 399). As Ophiôn and his consort were
deposed from power, so in turn was the Phoenician
Kronos by the Aryan Zeus. Mr. Farnell well
describes Kronos as ' one of the figures of a lost and
defeated religion ' (*Cults*, i. 25). But Homer, the
purely Aryan Hellene, who sang of the glory of
Hellas and her gods, took one view of his ultimate
fate, whilst Pindar, the Boiôtian, impregnated with
the Phoenician traditions of his country, took another.
Kronos thus degraded, a nocturnal Sun-god now
permanently confined to the Under-world, became a
figure of gloom and darkness, and is made to act like
the other Powers of the depth, the Gapers, Swallowers,
Hob-goblins of blackness and the Beneath. Lastly,
Kronos, as a god to whom human victims were offered
by Phoenician and Carthaginian down to a very late
period, became also from this circumstance still more
regarded as a Zeus Laphystios, a 'Glutton-god,' devourer of his offspring. The reader must bear in
mind that I am not here writing a treatise upon
Kronos, or on any of the mythic personages I may
mention; but merely giving in briefest outline the
standpoint from which their legends are regarded by
the Aryo-Semitic school. I have devoted two good-
sized volumes to Dionysos, and still there is a vast
amount to say about him; but, owing to the constantly increasing mass of material supplied by new
discoveries, which ever necessitates correction and
adjustment of views and suggestions, I have never
yet been able to bring out the intended third and concluding volume of the work. Art is too long and life

too brief for one man even to treat of the twelve chief
Hellenic divinities with anything like an exhaustive
completeness. He might almost as well attempt to
write the history of England on the scale of fullness
and thoroughness of a Freeman or a Gardiner. But,
I claim that the above view of the Kronos-myth, is the
only one which suggests any adequate interpretation
of its very singular and apparently absolutely conflicting details. And that the suggested etymon of his
name is simple, natural, not strained, and supported
alike by mythic incident and by linguistic example.
This cannot be said in favour of the conflicting
guesses of the Aryanists. Chronos ('Time') indeed
plays many singular tricks; but not such as are
ascribed to Kronos, son of Ouranos and sire of Zeus.
(For further notice of Kronos and the connected
horned divinities, vide R. B. Jr., *The Great Dionysiak
Myth*, II. Cap. IX. Sec. iii. *Taurokerôs*). At Olympia,
that great centre of divinities, still stands the Hill of
Kronos, though every temple is levelled to the ground;
and the ancient archives of the men of Êlis stated
that Kronos was first king in heaven, and had a
temple built to him at Olympia by the men of the
Golden Age (Paus. V. vii. 4).

XIV. Poseidôn

Prof. Müller, after remarking that one of the most
prominent features of the Vedic Sûrya (the Sun) and
Agni (Lat. Ignis), Fire, 'as dwelling in the sun,
consists in their triple character,' as representing the
rise, culmination, and setting of the sun; and that in the
Atharva-veda we meet with 'three welkins,' 'three
heavens,' three birth places of Agni' (*i.e.*, heaven,
earth, and clouds), etc., continues :—

' We find a similar division in Greece where the whole world is divided into three realms, the highest sky belonging to Zeus, the sea to Poseidon, and the lower world to Hades, these three sons of Kronos being originally personifications of the same Zeus ' (*C.* p. 657).

This passage affords an interesting example of the lengths to which the undue extension of a sound general theory can carry even the ablest men. Observe, first, that confusing together of things entirely distinct, which Bacon says is the mother of error. The triple character of Sûrya and Agni, as above mentioned, has nothing whatever to do, and offers no parallel, with the Homeric statement of Poseidôn (which I shall carefully consider) respecting the division of spheres of sway between the three Kronid brothers. As well might we say that the Vedic concept received illustration by the partition of empire between Octavius, Antony, and Lepidus. The extraordinary statement that ' these three sons of Kronos ' were originally but Zeus-Dyaus, Prof. Müller supports by reminding us that Haidês (poet. Aïdês, Aïdôneus, Lat. Hâdês) was called Zeus Katachthonios (Zeus ' of-the-Under-world '), and that Poseidôn was styled Zênoposeidôn. Just so; and I may add that Aischylos calls him θαλάσσιον Δία (' Zeus-of-the-sea '). And what, pray, is the force of such expressions? When the historian styles Wellington 'alike the Fabius and the Marcellus of the war,' does he mean that the Duke was a variant phase of those commanders? Or when the Japanese are referred to as ' the English of the Pacific,' are we to understand that in reality the two nations are but one? We find therefore no 'similar division in Greece.' 'But,' says Prof. Müller, in Greece 'the whole world is divided into three realms,' of which Zeus, Poseidôn and Haidês each take one. What a strange inaccuracy is here also! A division of 'the whole world' is just what we do *not* find in Greece. Let us turn to the Homeric statement itself, and observe that this declaration is put into the mouth of Poseidôn (not of Zeus or of Haidês), who is made to say thus :—

'Three brethren are we . . Zeus, and myself, and Hades is the third, the ruler of the folk in the under-world. And in three lots are all things divided, and each drew a domain of his own, and to me fell the hoary sea, . . and Hades drew the murky darkness, and Zeus the wide heaven, in clear air and clouds, *but the earth and high Olympus are yet common to all* (*Il.* xv. 187-93, ap. Lang). Thus 'the whole world' (= the All) was *not* divided between the three brothers.

Now we meet with this singular division of the All in no other Aryan mythology, and indeed in only one other mythology. We find it exactly in the archaic scheme of the Euphrates Valley. There Anu, Ak. Ana, takes the heaven, Bel the under-world and the darkness, and Êa (= Dagôn-Poseidôn) the deep. The earth was unappropriated and was common to all, and so was the Mountain of the World, on the summit of which the gods resided, and which Lenormant justly styles 'the Olympus of the Akkadians.' Here, then, is the origin of the arrangement to which appropriately Poseidôn has been made to appeal. He admits that Zeus, whose worship had been established in Greece long prior to his own, was 'the elder-born,' but charges him with undue interference, and says, ' Quietly let him abide in his third portion.'

The Aithiopians, *i.e.*, the 'Sun-burnt' inhabitants of the Phoenician littoral and of Libya (Cf. Hêrod. iv. 188), most distant of men from the standpoint of the Homeric poet, and separated by the empire of Egypt, into which Poseidôn could not gain admission (Vide *Ibid.* ii. 50), into two parts, one lying towards sunrise, the other towards sunset, are his special votaries. The god's contests with Athênâ have been noticed (*Sup.* p. 100) ; but they merely afford an instance amongst many such. Thus he contended unsuccessfully with Hêra for her favourite Argos; successfully with Zeus himself for the island of Aigîna; unsuccessfully with Dionysos for Naxos. At Delphoi and Korinth he submitted to arbitration, receiving the promontory of Taineron in Lakônikê for his Delphic rights or claims; and at Korinth being assigned the Isthmus, whilst Hêlios received the Akrokorinthos. To the Greeks he was especially a Sea-god, inasmuch as he had come to them across the sea; but that he was not a mere sea-god, such as their own Aryan Nêreus, is evident from a great variety of circumstances, *e.g.*, from the fact that his cult frequently obtained far inland. He is constantly contrasted by Homer with the great group of Aryan divinities, styled 'the gods who possess the wide heaven.' Opposed to them he is the 'Earth-possessing (Gaiêochos) Poseidôn;' they all pitied Odysseus, he did not (Vide *Od.* i. 19, 68). For further analysis of the Poseidônic myth I would refer the reader to my work *Poseidôn*, and to Mr. Gladstone's various and elaborate studies of the Homeric divinities.

XV. The Name 'Poseidôn'

Feeling Poseidôn slipping from his grasp, Prof. Müller makes one last desperate effort to retain his hold upon the god by supplying him with an Aryan name. This particular pathway is indeed marked by the traces of many a philological ruin; but, unless we are of those who deem that the commission of errors in any branch of study is good reason for abandoning it, we shall not merely be undiscouraged in such an enquiry, but derive much instruction from previous failures. The Professor, having noticed that 'much has been said in praise of a new [Aryan] etymology of Poseidôn' (*C.* p. 379) by Fick, proceeds practically to reject it, and intimates that Brugmann does the same. This cleared out of the way, we come to the point 'at grips,' as Mr. Lang would say. We are given an interesting list of dialectic variants of the god's name (Vide *C.* pp. 368, 399). It is found as the Aeol. Poseidan, the Ion. (tem. Hêrodotos) Poseideôn, the Arkad. Posoidan, the Lak. Pohoidan, the Thessal. Poteidoun, the Attic Poseidôn, the Epic Poseidâôn, the Boiot. Poteidâôn, the Old Dor. Potidan, Potîdas, etc. All these variants cannot be of the same age, and Prof. Müller insists : —

'That Poseidon is a later form of Potîdân, not *vice versâ*, cannot be doubted, as various inscriptions confirm this name, as well as the geographical name of Potîdaia' (*C.* p. 659).

How can any inscription prove that a variant occurring in it is the earliest form? Obviously it can only prove that such variant was in use at the time the inscription was written. That Doric colonists from the Isthmos who carried the cult of the god with them to their new Macedonian home (Vide Hêrod. viii. 129) on calling their foundation after him, should have used a Doric form of his name, proves nothing. What other kind of form would they have been likely to use? 'Potidæa,' says Leake (*Numis. Hel. in voc.*), 'the local form of Potidania or Posidonia, the city of Neptune.' I may remark in passing that Neptunus is entirely a distinct divinity from Poseidôn; but, it was formerly customary to call Greek divinities by Latin names, the original reason of the practice being that in the Middle Ages Western Europe did not understand Greek. Similarly, when an Achaian colony, Sybaris, founded a town and wished to name it after the god, they called it, not Potîdaia, but Poseidônia. So far, then, the question which was the older form remains an open one. Shall we take the Epic Poseidâôn and regard that as the original form? Why so? Prof. Müller is well aware, nay insists, that a shorter form may be quite as old as a longer one, Dêô as Dêmêtêr. Erechtheus as Erichthonios (Vide *C.* p. 368). And, again, are not words constantly altered syllabically by the poets to suit their own convenience? The Achaians and Athenians were chiefly Ionians, and in these variant forms we see mainly the Ionian σ opposed to the Doric τ, whilst the Attic Poseidôn is confirmed by the independent Aeol. Poseidan and Arkad. Posoidan. The late Ion. Poseideôn is merely a least-effort variant of the Epic form. Now Poseidôn was a special divinity of the Ionians, a sea-faring race from a remote period; and Ionian (Vide *sup.* p. 86) to Egypt and to the Semitic East, meant 'Greek.' It is, therefore, most probable that in the three very similar variants, Poseidan, Posoidan, and Poseidôn is contained the true and earliest Greek form of the god's name.

But, as Prof. Müller's argument proceeds, we see, why, without any sufficient cause, he insists that Potidân must be the oldest form of the name. He next asks :—' Might not his name Potîdas, Potîdân, Potîdâon, be explained as a dialectic form of Poti + îdaios, he who is near or against the wooded land or against Ida? . . . We actually have Poseidon's old name Potîdaios [What proof is there that this was his 'old name?'] preserved in the name of the town of Potîdaia ' (*C.* p. 659). If Prof. Müller can show the independent existence of the form *Potîdaios, we might admit that it reappears in Potîdaia. But, it seems, he cannot. As it happens, we have quite a group of variants of the name Poseidôn, but, alas, Potîdaios does not appear amongst them ; and the reason for this must be that there never was such a name. Potîdaia, instead of being founded on this phantom, will be, as Leake thought it was, an abraded form for Potîdanaia. Such abbreviations are constantly met with. But, with the disappearance of *Potîdaios vanishes likewise the extraordinary interpretation ' He-who-is-near-or-against-the-Wooded-land ' (Îda). This is explained by the suggestion that the Greeks always regarded Poseidôn (the sea) as at war with the land. They could not have thought thus, because, as we have seen, they knew that he shared the earth in

common with Zeus and Haidês. Nor are the shores
which to their knowledge he washed, by any means
particularly 'wooded.' If Poseidôn is Enosichthôn
('Shaker-of-the-land'), Dionysos is Elelichthôn
('Earth-shaker'); and the epithet has no necessary
connection with the sea. Ἴδα means 'a wood,' Ἴδη,
'the Wooded' hill; it does not in Greek mean
'wooded land.' But, yet, if anyone can accept this
remarkable etymon, one that, amongst other things,
leaves almost the entire history of the god unexplained
and unintelligible,—a circumstance which, on Prof.
Müller's own principles, justly condemns it,—if any
can still receive this hardest of sayings, let him
receive it. For my own part, I cannot but regard it
as equally unsupported by the philological facts of
the case, and by the general character of the
Poseidônic myth, as being forced and unnatural in
the highest degree, and therefore, as of course, quite
unreliable. It is a child of despair, the last arrow in
the Aryanistic quiver.

Let us next, in accordance with the entire bent
and indication of the Poseidônic myth, turn to a non-
Aryan-source; and observe what explanation of this
mysterious name presents itself. We have seen the
Fish-god pass westwards from the Euphratês Valley
to the Phoenician sea-board. We have seen him at
Athens at the birth of Erichthonios, still preserving
his unanthropomorphic form. Let us next catch this
old man of the sea at Krêtê a half-way house between
Phelesheth (Philistia) and Attikê. Says Lenormant:—

'Le nom d'un dieu *Tân* se trouve en composition
dans celui d'Itanos de Crête, *i-Tân*, "l'île de Tan."

Les plus anciennes monnaies de cette île représentent le dieu Tân comme un personnage á queue de poisson tenant le trident de Neptune [Exactly the same figure appears on coins of Ashqelôn, vide Babelon, *Monnaies des Perses Achém.* Pl. viii. No. 3] ; au revers est représenté le' monstre marin *tannín* et sa femelle' (*Les Origines*, i. 545, note 2).

The coinage of Itânos, of the fifth and fourth centuries B.C., shows this fish-tailed personage, who has been erroneously supposed to represent Glaukos, ' striking downwards with trident held in r. hand, and holding in l., fish.' The Rev. often shows ' two crested sea-monsters (*tanninîm*) facing one another ' (Wroth, *Brit. Mus. Cat. Gk. Coins of Crete*, etc. p. 51). So much for Itânos.

Turning to archaic Boiôtia, a district which was simply a mass of Phoenician influence, we find the eponymous Boiôtos described as the son of Itônos and the mymph Melanippê (Paus. IX. i. 1) *i.e.*, ' Black-horse ' = the Black-horse Dêmêtêr-Erinnys (Vide *sup.* p. 41). Now Poseidôn is specially the 'Lord' or ' Husband ' (Gk. *Posis*, Sk. *Patis*) alike of the Fish-goddess (Derketô, etc.) and of the Black-horse-god-dess. Thus Pindar (*Ol.* vi. 177-8), styles him Πόσις 'Αμφιτρίτας. Now compare the three forms Poseidan, Posoidan, and Poseidôn and I-tan-os, I-tôn-os with *Posis* prefixed ; and the result is Πόσις ῎Ιτανος = Ποσοιδάν, Ποσειδαν, Πόσις ῎Ιτωνος = Ποσειδῶν, *i.e.*, 'Lord-of-the-isle-of-Tan ' (Krêtê). Such, I believe, is the true interpretation of this very mysterious name ; and the reader will see how exactly it harmonizes with all that I have said about the god, and that neither philology nor meaning are in any way strained or unnatural. Poseidôn-Tan is thus Lord-of-the-Sea-monsters (*Tannînîm*) such as are shown on the Kretan coins; for 'many such pastureth the renowned Amphitrite' (*Od.* v. 422). I will conclude with words of the divine Homer:—

'The mighty Earthshaker . . . forthwith went down from the rugged hill, faring with swift steps, and the high hills trembled, and the woodland [Observe, the 'woodland' was not the only thing which trembled.] beneath the immortal footsteps of Poseidon as he moved [Mark, the god on land, not the sea, makes earth tremble.]. Three strides he made, and with the fourth he reached his goal even Aigae [*i.e.*, 'Goat-town,' Êa-Poseidôn, Elatês ('the Charioteer'), as the Athenians called him, being specially connected with the Goat, and as *Hêniochos-Auriga*, 'the starry Charioteer,' holding the *Goat, Aix-Capella*, Ak. *Askar*, 'Goat,' on his arm.], and there was his famous palace in the depths of the mere. . . Thither went he, and let harness to the car his horses swift of flight. . . and seized the well-wrought lash of gold, and mounted his chariot, and forth he drove across the waves. And the sea-beasts (*tannînîm*) frolicked beneath him, on all sides out of the deeps, for well they knew their lord' (*Il.* xiii. 17-28, ap. Lang).

XVI. Aphroditê

The extreme Aryanistic position of Prof. Müller is well illustrated by his resolute refusal to surrender Aphroditê, whose name he cannot explain, to the Semitic group of divinities. His argument is:—

' Homer calls Aphrodîte the Charis [Where? As frequently, Prof. Müller gives no reference, and this proposition is surely very dubious.], and as such the wife of Hêphaistos [Why must Charis be the wife of Hêphaistos? He suggests a natural phenomena explanation, but doubts it; observing, ' We must not attempt to explain too much.']. It is enough for us to know that Charis was Harit (morning splendour), just as she was Argynnis, the Sk. arguni, the bright, a name of the Dawn in the Veda' (C. p. 731).

I willingly admit the equations Charis = Harit, Argynnis = Argunî ; but this gets us no further. The syllogism is :—Charis was the wife of Hêphaistos: Aphrodîtê was the wife of Hêphaistos : therefore Charis = Aphrodîtê. This won't do. Mr. Gladstone well observes of Aphrodîtê :—

' We now know that the planetary worship of the Assyrians [and Babylonians, etc.] was brought by the Phoenicians into Greece [Thus, as Istar-Astartê was goddess of the ' Star of the morn and eve,' so to the Greeks Hesper-Phospher became the Star of Aphrodîtê.], and that each deity was associated with a particular metal. We find in Cyprus, the land of copper, with a Phoenician colony, the worship of Aphrodîtê. We may safely then refer the origin of this Olympian personage to the Assyrian [Say rather ' Euphratean,' as a wider term] mythology. The local indications of her worship, as proceeding from the [non-Aryan] East, are in accordance with the traditions which under the names of Astartè, Ashtoreth, Mylitta, exhibit to us a similar character as held in honour there.

The marriage with Hephaistos bears a similar witness; the more remarkable because it is only recognized in the mythology of the Outer-world, drawn from the Phoenicians, while in the Iliad he is the suitor of Charis' (*Juventus Mundi*, p. 315).

Mr. Gladstone then proceeds to admit the connexion of ‘the Charites . . with the Sanscrit Harits.’ In such an instance as that of Aphrodîtê, we cannot always begin *de novo*, repeating time after time arguments which have never been answered. We must appeal to the general concensus of scholars; and, as Mr. Farnell will probably not be suspected of undue leanings towards Semitism, I gladly call him as a witness. He gives a very long, learned, able, and almost exhaustive analysis of ‘Aphrodite-worship,’ regarded from the Hellenic side (*Cults*, ii. 618-730); and his general conclusions are as follows :—

1. Aphrodîtê was not an aboriginal Greek goddess.

2. She is nowhere in Greece regarded as autochthonous.

3. Her mythic adoption by Diônê is fictitious.

4. Her association with Hêphaistos, Arês, the Charites, etc., affords no proof of her Hellenic origin.

5. She is identical with ‘the Semitic goddess of Anterior Asia.’

6. Her maritime character is derived from the non-Aryan East.

7. She is identical with the armed and warlike goddess of the non-Aryan East, called by the Kyprians Aphrodîtê Encheios (Cf. ‘Of the-spear,’ Hêsychios).

8. Aphrodîtê Ourania = Sem. 'Aschthârth Melekhet Haschâmaîm (Cf. *Jer.* vii. 18, etc.).

9. Prof. Hommel's view of the name-change :— Ishtar - Ashtoret - Athtoret - Aphtoret - Aphrotet -'Aφρο-δίτη, is 'ingenious. . but philological analogies are wanting.'

At Athens, says Pausanias (I. xiv. 6) 'is a shrine of Aphrodîtê Ourania, who was first worshipped by the Assyrians, and after them by the Paphians of Kypros, and by the Phoenicians who dwelt at Askalôn in Palestine ; and from the Phoenicians the people of Kythêra learned her worship.' 'The shrine of Ourania' at Kythêra 'is the most holy, and of the temples of Aphrodîtê existing amongst the Greeks the most ancient' (*Ibid.* III. xxiii. 1).

Let this much suffice concerning Aphrodîtê.

XVII. 'Presenting Thebes'

The Theban mythic genealogy is as follows :—

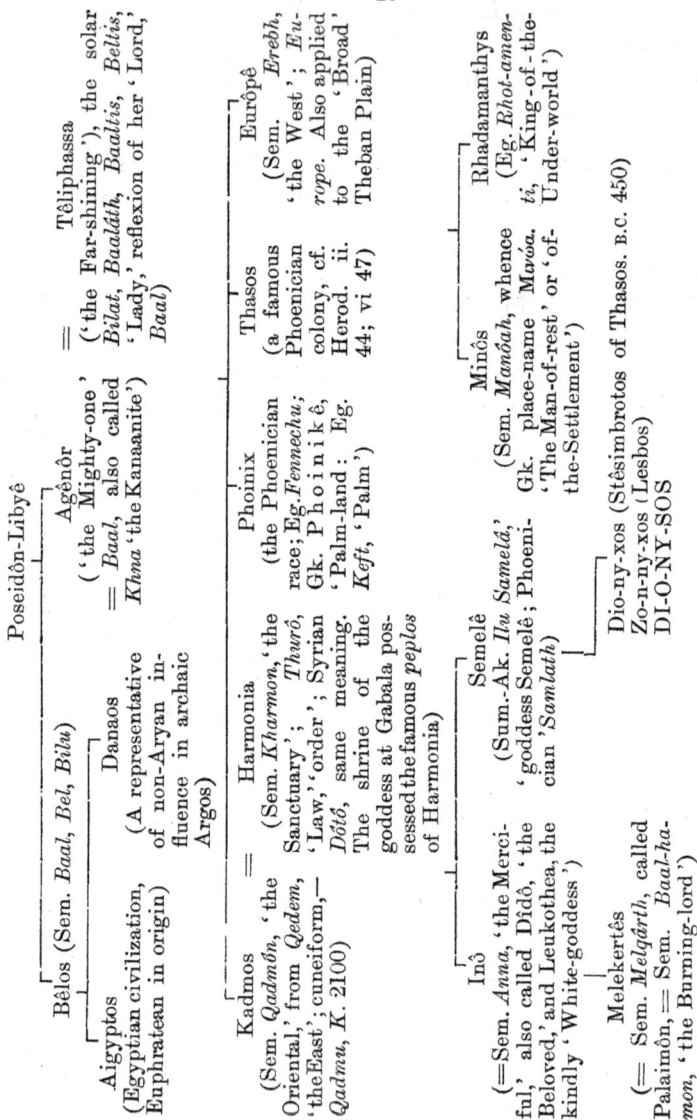

Poseidôn-Libyê

Bêlos (Sem. *Baal, Bel, Bilu*)

Agênôr ('the Mighty-one', = *Baal*, also called *Khna* 'the Kanaanite')

= Têliphassa ('the Far-shining'), the solar *Bilat, Baalâth, Baaltis, Beltis*, 'Lady', reflexion of her 'Lord', *Baal*)

Aigyptos (Egyptian civilization, Euphratean in origin)

Danaos (A representative of non-Aryan influence in archaic Argos)

Phoinix (the Phoenician race; Eg. *Fennechu*; Gk. P̂hoinik ê, 'Palm-land': Eg. *Keft*, 'Palm')

Thasos (a famous Phoenician colony, cf. Herod. ii. 44; vi 47)

Kadmos (Sem. *Qadmôn*, 'the Oriental', from *Qedem*, 'the East'; cuneiform,— *Qadmu, K.* 2100)

Europê (Sem. *Erebh*, 'the West'; *Eu-rope*. Also applied to the 'Broad' Theban Plain)

Kadmos = Harmonia (Sem. *Kharmon*, 'the Sanctuary'; *Thurô*, 'Law,' 'order'; Syrian *Dôtô*, same meaning. The shrine of the goddess at Gabala possessed the famous *peplos* of Harmonia)

Minôs (Sem. *Manôah*, whence Gk. place-name *Mινόα*. 'The Man-of-rest', or 'of-the-Settlement')

Rhadamanthys (Eg. *Rhot-amen-ti*, 'King-of-the-Under-world')

Inô (= Sem. *Anna*, 'the Merciful,' also called *Dîdô*, 'the Beloved,' and Leukothea, the kindly 'White-goddess')

Semelê (Sum.-Ak. *Ilu Samelâ*,' 'goddess Semelê; Phoenician 'Samlath)

Melekertês (= Sem. *Melqârth*, called Palaimôn, = Sem. *Baal-ha-mon*, 'the Burning-lord')

Dio-ny-xos (Stêsimbrotos of Thasos. B.C. 450)
Zo-n-ny-xos (Lesbos)
DI-O-NY-SOS

The name Dionysos.   The Ak. *di* means 'to judge,'
the Bab.-As. *dayan* is 'a judge,' Heb. and Ph. *dayon.*
Cf. 'Dan shall *judge* his people' (*Gen.* xlix. 16).   The
Bab-As. *nisu* is 'man,' Arab. *nâs,* 'human beings,'
an-nâs, 'the human race,' Heb. and Ph. *anoshim.*   In
the cuneiform inscriptions we find a title of the Sun-
god which is expressed in several variant forms.
Thus, in *W.A.I.* IV. xxviii. No. 1, l. 6, we read:—'*Ilu
Samas Da-ai-nu tsi-ru* ('The god the Sun, Judge
supreme').   In *W.A.I.* III. lxvi. Col. E. 1. 40, the
Tablet containing 'a list of gods in the temples of
Babylonia and Assyria,' we read:—'*Ilu Di-va-nu-kha*
[or *Ku'a*] *sa Ali* ('The god Divanukha of the City.'
Or 'the god the Judge of the Oracle of the City').
In *W.A.I.* II. lx. No. 2, l. 40, we read:—'*Ilu Dayan
rabû nis-i* ('The god the Great Judge of men'), who
is identified with Nabû (= Naβὼ. LXX.) who was
originally the Morning-sun (Vide Sayce, *Rel. Anct.
Babs.* p. 118).   Here we have a title of the Sun
Dayan-nisi ('Judge-of-men'), which would reappear
in Ph. as **Dayon anoshim.*   The Ph. Sacred Books,
etc., except the Fragments to which I refer in this
work, are lost.   Such a word as *nisi* or *noshi-m* would,
as part of the name of a single personage, to a Greek,
as of course, become *nysos;* and hence the origin of the
Gk. name Dionysos, which the Greeks themselves
ultimately not unnaturally thought signified 'the
Zeus of Nysa,' a mysterious locality which was placed
almost everywhere.   Such a form as *Divanukha,* if
that be the correct rendering, seems a suitable
source for the Thasian and Lesbian variants, Dionyxos.
From actual facts connected with the introduction of
his cult, to the Greeks Dionysos is primarily the
Sun-god who ripens the grape, and thus gives wine.

As Prof. Sayce has suggested, it is exceedingly probable that the cult of the god reached the Greeks, especially in Asia Minor, through the Hittites, as well as generally through the Phoenicians. The Dayannisi ' of the City ' of course = the Ph. Melekh-qiryath (Melqârth), and the ὁ τῆς πολέως θεὸς Διόνυσος, as the god was called at Teôs (Vide B. V. Head, *Brit. Mus. Cat. Gk. Coins of Ionia*, p. 317. On the name 'Dionysos,' Vide R. B. Jr., *The Great Dionysiak Myth*, ii. 207 *et seq.*). Prof. Müller alludes to the etymon of Dionysos proposed by Fox Talbot and myself, remarking :—

'This conjecture, however, is no longer accepted even by cuneiform scholars; no scholar now, I believe, approves of it ' (*C.* p. 218).

He is quite mistaken on this point. Thus, Mr. W. St. Chad Boscawen, the Assyriologist, when speaking about the title *Anax Andrôn*, remarks :—

'If, as Mr. Robert Brown, Jun. has shown so clearly, the origin of the Dionysiak Myth is to be found in the Chaldean solar epithet of *Dian nisi* (" Judge of men"),' may we not, etc. (*Babylonian and Oriental Record*, Dec. 1893, p. 94).

Speaking of the ' dukes ' of Edom, Prof. Sayce says :—

' Hadad was followed by Samlah of Masrekah (*Gen.* xxxvi. 36) or the " Vinelands," in whose name we discover that of a Phoenician god recorded in a recently found inscription, as well as that of the Greek Semelê. . . As the worship of Dionysos had been borrowed by the Greeks from the [non-Aryan] East, it has long been assumed that the name of Semelê must be of Phoenician extraction ; but it was only in 1884 that a Phoenician inscription was found in a bay to the west of the Peiraeos containing the name Pen-'Samlath ("the face of 'Samlath." ' *Rel. Anct. Babs.* p. 54).

Prof. Müller could hardly overlook this passage, and observes :—

' So long as there seemed to be some ground for supposing that the Aryan words for wine were derived from a Semitic language, there was some excuse for looking to a Semitic language for an explanation of the name of Dionysos or his mother Semele. But now that the evidence points clearly to an Aryan origin of οἶνος and vinum, even that excuse is gone ' (*C.* p. 217).

Is this so ? Curtius and Prof. Skeat (*Eng. Etymol. Dict. in voc.* Wine) remark :—

' It is only among the Graeco-Italians that we find a common name for the *grape* and its *juice*.'

Hehn, in his well-known and very valuable *Wanderings of Plants and Animals* (Eng. edit. by Stallybrass, p. 72) says :—

' That wine reached the Greeks through the Semites we learn from the identity of name (Heb. *yain,* Ethiop. and Arab. *wain,* Gr. *voinos,* Lat. *vinum*).'

He shows at length that the Semites could not have borrowed the word from the Graeco-Italians, and that the Iranians had it not.

Wharton, in his admirable *Etyma-Graeca*, 1882, gives, without the slightest hesitation ' (οἴνη vine, οἶνος wine (Lat. *vinum,* Got. *vein*): Heb. *yāyin*).'

' It is noticeable,' says Prof. Sayce, ' that the vine appears to have been first met with in Babylonia ' (*Assyrian Lects*. p. 152). Its Akkadian name is *gesdin* (' tree-of-life '). But I shall not pile up more authorities. The reader will see that there is excuse enough on this ground for looking to a Semitic language for an explanation of the names ' Dionysos ' and ' Semelê.'

But, continues Prof. Müller, because this Phoenician inscription has been found, therefore, it is stated, ' Semele, body and soul, is a corruption of the Phoenician 'Samlath.'

He knows better than this, but he is too impatient to consider the hated theory. He is well aware that this inscription is only one piece of evidence,—a very important one, I grant, neatly linking the Euphrates Valley with Hellas in the matter,—amongst an immense mass. He has often justly resented such treatment of his own identifications, when some careless person made his whole case rest on this or that point, ignored everything else, and, lastly, derided him.

He continues :—' How 'Samlath became Semele is hardly asked.'

No, because it is so obvious :—The Ak. *Samelâ*, passing into a Semitic language, would take the feminine *t*, becoming in Assyro-Babylonian *Samelat* (Cf. Bila-*t*, Zarpani-*t*, Tasmi-*t*, etc.), whence the Phoenician 'Sam-lath. But the Greek does not allow female names ending in θ. Hence the equation 'Sa-m(e)-la(th) = Gk. Σεμέλη. What is amiss here? And yet Prof. Müller solemnly warns Prof. Sayce and other innocents that, at this rate, 'we shall soon drop back into the days when Jovis was derived from Jehovah.' Really this sort of thing tends to become ridiculous.

But if the names of Kadmos and Semelê are not only Semitic, but even appear in the cuneiform records, we need not be surprised to find the name of Dionysos, grandson of the one and son of the other, in the Babylonian inscriptions. As regards the other chief name of the god, I have shown, and supported each step by examples, that Melqârth ('the City-king') = Bakchos, the transitional forms being *M-l-q-r-t*, *M-l-q-r*, *B-k-r*, *B-k-o*. If anyone is, *primâ facie*, inclined to dispute this, let him first study Gesenius, and then read the section in my book on the name ' Bakchos.'

Years ago Prof. Sayce wrote to me :—

' I think that your Dionysos has now become part of our scientific heritage. You proved your view so completely that it is now accepted on all sides as a matter of course.'

Prof. Müller's book had not then been written. But cannot he, with his vast knowledge, suggest an Aryan etymon for ' Dionysos.' No, strange to say, he cannot. He once made a suggestion in a former work ; but as it does not appear in *C.*, I will not refer to it. Prof. Bechtel's amusing effort has been noticed (*Sup.* p. 16).

Like Poseidôn, Dionysos is unanthropomorphic, Dikerôs, Kerasphoros, Keratophuês, Kerôs, Pyri-phengês, Pyrôpos, Stylos (' the Pillar '), Taurokerôs, Taurometôpos, Tauromorphos, Taurophuês, Taurôpos, etc., the horned, radiant and burning Sun-god, the

bull-headed Dionysos Hyês=the Ox-headed (statue
of) Molekh. In Élis, the land of Êl, he was regarded
as the Sun (*Etymol. Meg.* in voc. *Dionysos*); and to
him sang the women :—

Ἐλθεῖν, ἥρω Διόνυσε,
ἀγνὸν σὺν Χαρίτεσσιν,
τῷ βοέῳ ποδὶ θύων
ἄξιε ταῦρε, ἄξιε ταῦρε.

Ἀλείων ἐς ναόν
ἐς ναόν

(Plut. *Kephal. Katag. Hellen.* xxxvi. 7).

No Bull-totem, my masters, remember. We have
got rid of that (Vide *sup.* p. 70).

The kosmic Sun-god, as of course, is a Vegetation-
god, Lord of Growth, but to limit him to this, to
turn him into a mere Corn-spirit, is puerile.

I am indebted to Prof. Sayce for the above interpretation of Minôs. The name is unconnected with
the Eg. Mena, or with Aryan *man* and *mind* words.

No Aryan etymon of the name 'Thêbai' is
possible. The Egyptian Thebes (= Tâpê, Thâpâ,
'the Head') is unconnected; but the instance shows
a non-Aryan derivation of the same Greek-formed
name. There was a Thêbê in Mysia, and the
Palestinian town-name Thebez (*Jud.* ix. 50), may
possibly be an allied form. From Homer and
Hêsiod downwards the first prominent features
connected with the Boiôtian Thebes are its seven
gates, which have ever been justly associated with
Semitic planetary worship. Without accepting every
detail given by the very learned Nonnos (v. 64 *et seq.*),
we may undoubtedly admit the general principle.
Planetary symbolism in art had been practised in the
East from a remote antiquity. Thus the ornamenta-
tion of the walls of Ekbatana (Hêrod. i. 98) was
probably derived from that of the Temple of the

Seven Spheres (Planets) at Barsipki (Borsippa) near Babylon, the seven stages of which, beginning at the base, were coloured Black for Ninip-Samdan ('the Powerful')-Îl-Kronos-*Saturn*, Orange for Marduk (= Merôdach)-Baal-Zeus-*Jupiter*, Red for Nergal-Melekh (= Moloch)-Arês-*Mars*, Golden (thin gold plates were actually used) for Samas-Melqârth-Êlektôr-*Sol*, pale Yellow for Istar-Gîddê (Cf. *Gad*, god-of-good-luck, Is. lxv. 11)-Aphrodîtê-*Venus*, Blue for Nabû (= Nebô)-Taût-Hermês-*Mercury*, and Silver for 'Aschthârth-Mênê-Selênê-*Luna*.

The arrangement of the city of Thebes is exactly in harmony with all this. We know from the testimony of Dikaiarchos, who visited it, cir. B.C. 290, shortly after its rebuilding by Kassandros on the old lines, that it was 'circular'; and we learn from Armenidas (ap. Souidas) that the Kadmeia or Akropolis was styled Μακάρων νῆσοι (' The Isles of the Blessed'). This is clearly a mystical title, and the general kosmic symbolism of the place makes it possible that its name may really be the Sem. *Têboh*, Arab. *tâbût*, the ark, shrine, sacred spot—of the Makarians, *i.e.*, the followers of Dionysos-Melqârth, which latter title appears all about the Mediterranean coast in such forms as Makar, king of Lesbos ; Makaria, ancient name of Lesbos and of Rhodes, and name of a town of Kypros ; Makaria, daughter of Hêraklês-Melqârth, who, in true Phoenician style, was sacrificed in order that a victory might be obtained, and who gave her name to a fountain at the Phoenician settlement of Marathôn (Paus. I. xxxii. 5 ; vide *sup.* p. 100) ; Makara, a town of Sicily ; Makaraia, a town of Libya; etc. The gates of the whole inclosure, including the Lower City which is that stated (*Od.* xi. 263) to have been founded by Amphiôn ('the Daily-sun.' Prof. Müller.) and Zêthos (for whose name there is no Aryan etymon. Cf. such Sem. names as Zêtham, 1 *Chron.* xxiii. 8), exactly correspond in order with the planetary arrangement of the Borsippa Temple. The First or Northern Gate was dedicated to the Horned-moon, 'Aschthârth-Astartê-Mênê. It was also called the Hypsistan Gate, because near it stood a temple of Zeus Hypsistos (= Sem. Êl-'Eliôn, *Gen.* xiv. 22, 'God - most - high,' the 'Ελιοῦν of Sanchouniathôn, i. 5. So Hêsychios : 'Ελιεύς· Ζεὺς ἐν Θήβαις). The Second or North-eastern Gate looked towards Chalkis and was dedicated to Hermês, = (as analogue) the Ph. Taût, 'whom the Greeks called Hermês (Sanch. i. 4). Taût = (as analogue) the Bab. Nabû ('the Proclaimer'—of the Sun, primarily the Sun himself, vide *sup.* p. 133), god of the planet *Mercury.* As the Gk. Hermês was (wrongly) supposed to = the Lat. Mercurius, we, on account of this string of (practical, not philological) equations, call the little planet *Mercury.* The Third or Eastern Gate was dedicated to the armed Aphrodîtê (For thirteen instances of her Hellenic cult, vide Farnell, *Cults,* p. 749), who represents (an original) Istar of the Morning-star, goddess of war, who formed a Diad with Istar of the Evening-star, goddess of love. At Thebes this armed Aphrodîtê, Encheios ('Spear'-goddess), was called Onka ('the Burning.' Vide Bérard, *Cultes Arcad.* p. 140, for the authorities, and for nine instances of this name-formation in Boiôtia and Arkadia, two localities which constantly present parallels. Semelê was also known as Enchô. Hêsych. in voc.). Being a warlike goddess, the Greeks

naturally called her Athêna. Pausanias (IX. xii. 2)
expressly states that Onka was a Phoenician word.
Maury refers to the ' Minerva virtus solis ' (Macrob.
Sat. i. 17). The Fourth or Southern Gate, the road
from which led to Plateia, was called ' the Êlektran,'
and dedicated to the Sun (Êlektôr), Bab.-As. Samas-
Dayan-nisi, Ph. Shemesh-Melqârth, Gk. Bakchos-
Dionysos. The Phoenician divinity Eschmûn, eighth
and highest of the Kabîrîm, also appears at Thebes
and in his solar phase (Vide *sup.* p. 111). To the
Greeks he became Apollôn Ismênios. The Fifth
or Western Gate was dedicated to the War-god, the
Bab.-As. Nergal ('the Strong'), originally god of
death and the Under-world, and thus placed on the
side of Erebos (Darkness), the Phoenician Usâv or
Uschô (Gk. Ousôös)-Harekhal, Gk. Arês-Hêraklês,
Lat. *Mars.* As Schroeder and Lenormant have
proved, a form such as the Gk. Ou-sôös represents an
original Bo-sôös (*e.g.,* Ph. *Bo-dam* = Gk. *Ou-dam*),
and *Bo* is a contraction of *Bar* (*e.g.,* ' *Bo*-milcar pro
Bar-milcar '). Hence, Bosôös = Ph. Bar-sav (Cf.
Heb. Êsâv), ' the Son-of-hair', = ' the Hairy-one,'
Ousôös, ' who was the first who made clothes of the
skins of animals which he slew . . . and was the
first who launched a boat ' (Sanch. i. 3), Hêraklês
in his lion's skin, sailing westward to his Pillars in
the golden solar boat-cup. Another great solar hero
is a variant phase of this concept ; the Ph. *Bar-sav*
= Gk. *Per-seus,* whose name in Greek might mean
' Destroyer,' and who delivers Andro-meda, Ph.
Adâm-mâth ('the Rosy,' *i.e.,* ' Beautiful '), daughter
of Kêpheus (= Ph. Kêph, the heavenly ' Stone,'
Aramaic *Kêphas*), the Phoenician Baitulos (= Ph.
Bêthêl), ' the Living-stone' ; for the god Schâma

(= Gk. Ouranos) endowed certain βαιτύλια with souls
(Sanch. i. 6.). The myth reappears at Thebes,
where, as Amphiôn plays on his *phorminx heptatonos*
('seven-stringed harp,' the seven tones corresponding
with the seven planets), the 'lively stones' rise and
form the city wall (Paus. IX. v. 4).

The Sixth or North Western Gate was dedicated
to the Bab. Bilu-Maraduku (= Bel-Merôdach), Ph.
Baal, Gk. Zeus-Bêlos, Lat. Jupiter. My meaning in
making these comparisons will not, I presume, be
misunderstood. The equation between Bel and Baal,
on the one hand, and Zeus and Jupiter on the other
is not that they are identical concepts or philological
variants ; but simply that they are the corresponding personages in the several Pantheons. It was
because the Babylonians had connected their chief
god with the planet *Jupiter*, that the Greeks connected their chief god (Zeus) with it.

The Seventh or N.N.W. Gate of Thebes was
dedicated to the Babylonian god whose name was
formerly read as Adar, but who is now provisionally
called Nin-ip. One title of his, Uras ('the Veiled-
one') is quite certain. He reappears westward as the
Phoiniko-Greek Îl-Kronos, identified (wrongly) with
the Lat. Saturnus. He is the Ph. Schamê-mêrum
(= Gk. Samêmroumos), whose name is translated
by Philôn as Hypsouranios ('the High-celestial'),
i.e., in a planetary phase, *Saturn*, highest of the
planets. This planet, Ak. Ginna ('Commander,'
'leader'), in Bab.-As. is Ka-ai-wa-nu, or Ka-ai-nu, Ph.
Kîyûn (Chiun. Amos, v. 26), Hittite Kên, 'the Pillar '
(Cf. Dionysos Stylos) whence the Gk. κίων. The
Phoenician pillar-cult is familiar. The two pillars
which Hêrodotos (ii. 44) describes at the temple of

Hêraklês-Melqârth at Tyre, the pillars of Solomon's temple, the two obelisks of Egyptian temples, the two minarets of the modern mosque supply connected examples.

As the forms of Vedic divinities are often shadowy, glide into each other and coalesce, so do the variant god-phases of the Eastern Mediterranean. The original idea in each case, could we reach it, is always natural, simple, logical. The development by many minds of many nations often produces apparent confusion, discord and contradiction.

Says Lenormant :—

' Dans le personnage de Cadmus, deux idées, deux-figures distinctes se fondent en une seule. Cadmus est en même temps *l'oriental*, le chef de la principale colonie phênicienne en Grèce, *et l'un des dieux* dont le culte fut apporté par cette colonie [The Diad of god and god-introducer.]. Aussi, à Sparte ex à Thèbes, Cadmus est il honoré comme une divinité. Dans les mystères phénico-pelasgiques de Samothrace, un des Cabires se nomme *Cadmus* ou *Cadmilus*, corrompu ensuite en *Casmilos* et *Camillos*.' Kadmilos = Qedem-el (= 'qui coram Deo stat'), a title which includes the ideas 'd'un dieu ministre ou démiurge, et d'une manifestation extérieure de la divinité suprême' (*Les Prem. Civ.* ii. 322). This Samothracian Kadmilos being thus the *administer* of the Kabîrîm, is called Hermês by the Alexandrian grammarian Dionysid-ôros; so we find that 'Tuscos Camillum appellare Mercurium' (Macrob. *Sat.* iii. 8). According to the Alexandrian grammarian Mnaseas, the chief Kabeiric triad consisted of personages whom he calls Axieros (— Zeus. *Schol.* Apollon. Rhod.), Axiokersos (==

Dionysos. *Ibid.*), and Axiokersê (=Aphrodîtê.Skopas), with Kasmilos as their assistant. It is a curious fact that in *W.A.I.* III. lvii. No. 2,1. 2-5, we find four stars called *Kas-mi-lu*, *Kas-u-zu-gur* (*lacuna*), *Kas-si-ki-su*, and *Kas-sa*. It may be that Kasmilos is not a corruption of Kadmilos, but an independent word; and, without any dogmatism in the matter, it almost seems as if we had here the following equations :—
Kasmilu = *Kasmilos*; *Kasuzugur* = *Axioker* (*sos*) ; *Kassikisu* = *Axiokersê*; and *Kassa* = *Axier*(*os*). In Ak. *Kas* means 'double.' If each of these are diads, the combination might perhaps represent the eight Kabîrîm, the seven + Eschmûn. I will not pursue the enquiry here; but the judicious reader will observe that an exhaustive knowledge of the cuneiform remains would probably enable us to clear up very many obscurities (For further consideration of the subject, vide R. B. Jr., *The Great Dionysiak Myth*, ii. 212 *et seq.*).

XVIII. A Semitic Moon-myth

Opposed to the dark, mourning and chthonian goddess of the Semites who appears in Hellas now as Dêmêtêr Melainê (Vide *sup*. p. 41) and again as Aphrodîtê Melanis (Paus. II. ii. 4), etc. is the ' Reine de la lumière, l'Ourania-Korè-Soteira une déesse blanche' (Bérard, *Cultes Arcad*. p. 182, where many references to the Semitic Leukothea are collected). The cult of Inô was well known in Greece. Near Megara was shown the rock whence tradition said she had leapt into the sea with her child Melikertês (=Melikarthos, Philôn's transliteration of Melqârth or Melqârt) to avoid the fury of her husband Athamas

Paus. I. xliv. 11). In the temple óf Palaimôn (= Sem. Baal-hamon) at Korinth stood statues of Poseidôn, Inô-Leukothea and Melikertês-Palaimôn himself (*Ibid.* II. ii. 1). Not far from the promontory of Maleia was the Lake of Inô, near which her festival was kept. The goddess (= the Moon) was regarded as the nurse of Dionysos (= the young Sun of the next day. *Ibid.* III. xxiv. 3). Not far from Korônê in Messênia, and near the seashore, was a temple of Inô at a place where the goddess was said to have landed, and where she was worshipped under the name of Leukothea (*Ibid.* III. xxxiv. 2).

It is Homer who pourtrays her in her most charming aspect. As the luckless Odysseus is tossed to and fro on his raft in the darkness, for the poet specially notices that ' down sped night from heaven,' the daughter of Kadmos marked him, fair-ankled Inô (= the Moon walking in brightness), and gave him her veil divine (= the line of moon-light) to wind around his breast as help and guidance to him on his way. Of course he could not retain this head dress; the moon would take her light with her when she went. And so we read that when he reached safety, he let the veil fall from him, 'and quickly Inô caught it in her hands' (*Od.* v. 461-2).

XIX. Athamas = Tammuz

The gentle Moon-goddess, mother or nurse of next day's sun, Melikertês or Dionysos, must fly from her mate, the raging Sun-god. So to avoid her husband Athamas (= Hêraklês Mainomenos), driven mad by the hostile Aryan goddess Hêrê, Inô, as we have

10

seen, sinks in the sea. This alternate flight and
pursuit of Sun and Moon has given rise to the famous
story of the contest between the Lion (= Sun) and
the Unicorn (= Moon. Vide R. B. Jr., *The Unicorn*);
and also to another very curious myth, preserved in
all its details in heraldic legend, viz., the flight of the
Leopard (= Stars) from the Lion, and the subsequent devouring of the latter by the former, when
the noble beast has got stuck fast in the narrow
entrance of the Leopard's cave, *i.e.*, in the dark
narrow passage leading to the Under-world. Athamas,
'in Ionic Tammas' (K. O. Müller, *Orchomenos und
die Minyer*, p. 156), and hence the *a* is prosthetic, and
the name is unconnected with the Aryan root *ath*, is
son of Aiolos ; and 'everything combines to raise
the presumption about the Phoenicianism of the
Aiolids, to the rank of a rational conclusion' (Gladstone, *Juv. Mun.* p. 137). The god of Athamas was
the Phoenician Kronos-Melekh, Zeus Laphystios ('the
Gluttonous,' *i.e.*, desirous of human sacrifices), whose
cult obtained amongst the Minyai (= the men of
Minôs and the Minôa, vide *sup.* p. 132), who had
established an archaic civilization at Iolkos (Vide *inf.*
p. 194) and in northern Boiôtia. The principal
τέμενος ('sacred enclosure') of this divinity was not
far from Koroneia ; and there, according to the
legend, Athamas, like a true Phoenician, was about
to sacrifice his Aryan children Phrixos and Hellê to
the Laphystian Zeus, when they were rescued by
the Golden Ram (Paus. IX. xxxiv. 4). This Ram,
the 'pecus Athamantidos,' was always identified
with the zodiacal *Aries*, which figure, as I have
abundantly proved elsewhere, is a stellar reduplication of the original golden solar Ram, alike famous

in Babylonia, Egypt, or India. Now whenever in
Greek legend we meet with one of the ancient
constellation-figures, there is Phoenician influence.
Pausanias (I. xxiv. 1) is quite aware that 'the god
who is called Laphystios among the Orchomenians,'
was not a Hellenic divinity. The human-sacrifice-cult
which obtained amongst the supposed descendants
of Athamas in connexion with the Laphystian Zeus,
is very familiar from the account in Hêrodotos (vii.
197) ; and I may observe that there is no real
evidence that human sacrifices were ever offered by
any archaic Greeks entirely untouched by Semitic
influence. M. Bérard has absolutely demonstrated
by a most elaborate investigation of locality, art,
ritual and names, that Zeus Lykaios, to whom such
sacrifices were undoubtedly offered, was the Phoenician Baal; and, as such, identical with Zeus
Laphystios. Take another instance. Just before
the battle of Salamis Euphrantidês, the soothsayer,
insisted that three beautiful captives on the galley of
Themistoklês should be sacrificed to Bakchos Ômêstês
('the Devourer-of-raw-flesh,' = Zeus Laphystios).
Themistoklês ' was astonished at the strangeness and
cruelty of the order,' but the highly excited Athenian
sailors insisted on its being carried out (Plut. *Themis.*
xxiii). Here is an illustration alike of the Phoenician character of Dionysos, and of the lingering force
of archaic cruel superstitions, Phoenician in origin,
stung into a last spasm of hateful life in that awful
moment when the existence of a nation trembled in
the balance. When we meet with statements about
human sacrifices in late authors, *e.g.*, Porphyry, the
first question to be considered is, Of what divinity
is he speaking ? If Artemis be named, who is really

10 *

meant by Artemis?   She probably will not be the
Aryan sister of Apollôn; and whatever Porphyry
himself may have thought on such a point is quite
immaterial.   Mr. Hogarth, in a remarkable passage
on the Thebans of the fourth century B.C., observes:—

'The Cadmeian characteristics are those of a conquering people of the East. . . The Cadmeian was
an alien in Boeotia in a far more real sense than the
Dorian Spartan among the earlier races of the
Peloponnese . . The familiar legends of Thebes are
as gloomy as the horrible nature myths of the East.
Œdipus; the man-eating Sphinx ; Agave and her
hideous orgy ; Dirce tied to the wild bull's horns—
all these forms of horror find parallels in Thrace,
Phrygia or Phoenicia rather than in Hellas.   Even
in 371 the Theban commanders at Leuctra could
debate the propriety of offering human sacrifice to
the unpropitious gods ' (*Philip and Alex. of Macedon*,
pp. 34-5 ; vide Plut. *Pelop.* xxi).

The foregoing considerations, with much other
evidence, long since made it clear to me that
Athamas-Tammas = Tammuz-Adoni (' My Lord,'
Gk. Adônis), the familiar Sun-god of Syria (*i.e.*, the
Land of the Suri.   Vide Hommel, *Anct. Heb. Trad.*
p. 210) and Phoenicia.   In Nov. 1883 Prof. Sayce,
than whom no one is more qualified to give an
opinion on such a question, wrote congratulating me
on my discovery ' that Athamas is Tammuz'; and
in his *Herod.* (p. 97) refers to 'the Phoenician legend
of Athamas or Tammuz, the Sun-god.'   The Ak. Sun-
god Duwu-zi (' Son-of-life'), a name understood by
the Semites as meaning ' the Only-son,' became
with them Timmuz or Tammuz ; and the loves of

Istar and Duzu (the shortened form of the god's name), were reduplicated in those of Aphrodîtê and Adônis. The 'weeping for Tammuz' (Ez. viii. 14) began with the Phoenician cry *Ai-lênu* (' Alas for ‧ us !' Gk. αἴλινος.), the dirge, personified as Linos.

XX. Kirkê

In a special monograph (*The Myth of Kirkê*) I have minutely considered the history of this Homeric Moon-goddess of the Outer-world, Kirkê (' the Round ' = the Full-moon) of ' the Aiaian isle '; and have shown that Aia, the moon-island, is a reduplication of the Moon-goddess, 'own sister to the wise and terrible Aiêtês' (*Od.* x. 137) = Lunus. Instances of this Turanian (by which I mean non-Aryan and non-Semitic) moon-name are as follows :—

Ak. *A*, *Aa*, the Moon-goddess (Cf. Eg. *aâh*, 'moon'), *I-du* (' the Goer,' a name corresponding with the Aryan moon-name Iô, ' the Goer'), which appears in Hêsychios as 'Αἴδώ, 'Αἴδης· ἡ σελήνη παρὰ Χαλδαίοις. 'Αἴδης = 'Αιήτης, mythic king of Kolchis, and son of Hêlios. Luna is 'own-sister' to Lunus. As.-Turkic, Osmanli *Ai*, Siberian Tatars *ay*, Ostiak *i-re*, Taugy *i-ri*, Tomskoi-Ostiak *i-rraen*, Buriat *ha-ra*, Samoied *ji-ry*, *e-ra*, Ak. *i-tu, i-du*, 'month,' Etruscan *ai-vil* (= *annus*, as moon-marked), Et.-Lat. *i-tis*, *i-tus*, ' the half month, time of the half-moon,' *i-dus*, *i-du-lis*, the sheep sacrificed at the Ides. I presume it will now be admitted, after the researches of Canon Is. Taylor, Prof Pauli, and others, that Etruscan is a non-Aryan language (Vide R. B. Jr., *The Etruscan Numerals*, 1889).

That the Kirkê-myth is entirely Euphratean in origin, is fully proved in my book ; and is quite

admitted by Prof. Sayce, who says, ' Your com-
parison of the myth of Kirkê with that of the
lovers of Istar is as self-convincing as your discovery
that Athamas is Tammuz' (Vide *sup.* p. 148).
Mr. Gladstone, whose acuteness had discerned in
the Homeric Kêtaioi, the people called by the
Egyptians Kheta, and by the Assyrians Khatti, *i.e.*,
the Hittites, saw at once how well a Euphratean
origin of the Kirkê tale harmonized with all the
Homeric and other facts of the case, and wrote,
' I hail the doctrine that Kirkê is Euphratean.' The
book was also warmly commended by Prof. Tiele,
an authority whose praise is especially valuable ;
and I mention these circumstances because, as
noticed (*sup.* p. 31), this monograph was fiercely
attacked and its statements gravely misrepresented.

The Homeric poems supply many instances of the
use of non-Aryan names and words, *e.g.* :—Aia,
Aiêtês, Aigyptos (= Eg. Ha-Ka-Ptah, ' House-of-the-
worship-of-Ptah.' Brugsch.), Aphrodîtê, Assarakos
(= Assôr-akhu, ' Assôr is my protector '), Dardanos
(Cf. As. Tartan, ' Commander-in-chief '), Dionysos,
Erebos, Ilos (= Ilu, Îl, Êl), Kadmos, Kêteioi,
Kimmerioi (= the Gimirraai, whose country
was N.E. of Assyria), Kiôn (= the Sem. Pillar-god,
Dionysos-Stylos, Zeus-Meilichios, who was repre-
sented at Sikyôn in pyramidal form, whilst by him
was the statue of the Semitic goddess called Artemis
Patrôa, Paus. II. ix. 6, ' Belonging-to-one's-father-
land,' set up by some Phoenician immigrant),
Kronos, Ôrîôn (Vide *inf.* p. 172), Poseidôn, Rhada-
manthos, Sarpedôn (= 'the Sapardian'), Thêbê,
Thêbai, *chalkos* (= Sem. *châlâk*, ' smooth '), *chrusos*
(= Sem. *kharouts*, As. *khuratsu*, ' gold '), *krokos*

(= Sem. *karkôm*), *kyparissos* (= Sem. *kopher*), *leôn*, Kretan *lis* (= Sem. *layish*), *phykos* (= Sem. *pouk*, ' tangle '), etc.

XXI. The Homeric 'Nekyia'

From Kirkê' to the Nekyia is a natural transition, and it is now generally acknowledged that, not merely is the whole tone and presentation of the Under-world in *Od*. xi. un-Hellenic,—although of course grandly adorned by the splendour of Greek genius and the beauty of Greek feeling,—but that this gloomy realm is actually identical with the Euphratean Under-world and with the Scheôl of Phoenician and Hebrew, so vividly brought before us in the Old Testament.   For detailed examination of the various points and incidents in the visit of Odysseus to Hadês, I would refer the reader to Gladstone, *Homeric Synchronism* (1876), p. 219 *et seq*., and to my *Myth of Kirkê*, p. 96 *et seq*. ; and will here mainly confine myself to the question in its general form.   I am happy to be able to quote Prof. Müller as being in harmony with the above view. In his *Anthropological Religion* (1891), Lect. xi. ' Soul after Death,' speaking on this subject, he says :—

' The Nekyia does *not* represent the popular [Greek] belief. . . . The Homeric poems are a splendid fragment, but they are a fragment only of ancient Greek thought. . . . Many scholars in describing to us what the ancient Greeks thought about life after death, have taken [the] Nekyia for their chief, nay for their only guide.   But this very rhapsody has by some excellent critics been considered as very peculiar and exceptional, and as being possibly the work of a different, probably a Bœotian poet. . . . Homer does not reflect popular opinion on death.'

As to what we ought rightly to understand by the name ' Homer,' and on the question of the authorship of *Od*. xi., I give no opinion here; suffice it to note that Prof. Müller is fully aware of the un-Hellenic tone and character of the relation, and that he specially connects it with Boiôtia, *i.e.*, practically with Phoenicia. We see how deeply Boiôtia had stamped her special influence on both Homer and Hêsiod, as we know them.

Looking then at the Homeric account in a general way, we observe that king Odysseus, like king Saul, would consult the shade of a majestic prophet respecting his future destiny. He reaches the appointed spot, performs the appropriate ritual, and ' anon came the soul of Teirêsias with a golden sceptre in his hand.' He knows Odysseus, remembers the past, foretells the future, and then ' went back within the house of Hadês,' which is described as ' a land desolate of joy,' where dwell ' the strengthless heads of the dead,' 'phantoms of men outworn.' ' All go unto one place ' (*Ec*. iii. 20), Teirêsias, Achilleus, Tantalos ; good, bad and indifferent, great and small, Samuel, Saul, Jonathan. True there are divisions in this place, as indicated alike in the legend of the Descent of Istar, and in the account of Dives and Lazarus. In the Hadês of the *Nekyia* there is a sort of penal settlement, where Sisyphos and other great offenders are tormented ; and there is some gulf or gap betwixt them and 'the mead of asphodel,' where dwell the shades of the great heroes and their attendants. This dread part of Hadês recalls the Abaddôn ('Place-of-destruction') of the Old Testament. 'Scheôl and Abaddôn are before Yahveh' (*Prov.* xv. 11), *i.e.*, 'Scheôl is naked before Him and Abaddôn hath no covering' (*Job*, xxvi. 6); and they 'are never full' (*Prov.* xxvii. 20). Yet there is room. And 'the Dead know not anything' (*Ec.* ix. 5) that is happening in the Upper-world. Agamemnôn and Achilleus would fain hear from Odysseus of the doings of their sons. The writer of *Ecclesiastes* does not mean that the Dead do not exist ; but those who pass 'the gates of Scheôl' (Is. xxxviii. 10), the Rephaîm (*Ps.* lxxxviii. 10), *i.e.*, 'Weak-ones,' become 'strengthless.' Therefore Scheôl cannot praise Yah (*Ib.* cxv. 17), a name which $=$ the Bab. Yâ, as Yahveh, Yahweh$=$Bab. Yâwa (Vide T. G. Pinches, in *Proc.* Soc. Bib. Archaeol. Nov. 1892, p. 19 *et seq.*; Hommel, *Anct. Heb. Trad.* pp. 113, 145); for, it is a rule 'since man was placed upon earth' that 'he shall fly away as a dream, and shall not be found' (*Job*, xx. 4, 8); or, as Antikleia says in the *Nekyia*, 'The spirit like a dream flies forth.' She herself flits from the hands of Odysseus 'as a shadow or even as a dream'; and the shades of the Suitors pass 'as bats flit gibbering in the secret place of a wondrous cave,' which Scheôl is. The Homeric picture of Scheôl was limned centuries prior to the Captivity; it was not borrowed from the Babylonia of Nebuchadrezzar the Great. And when Ezekiel (xxxii.) draws his weird dark scene of Scheôl-Hadês, to which the kings and multitudes of Egypt, Assur, Elam, and other neighbouring nations were to descend, and where, like Agamemnôn and Achilleus, they converse, he, a priest of Israel, one who has been styled a ' High Churchman,' had not abandoned at a moment's notice his own national belief and accepted that of Babylonia. He merely gave utterance to the faith which he and his people had shared for centuries, alike with Babylonia and with the other nations of Western Asia, for all of whom this Nekyia-Scheôl was an undoubted article of faith. The same remark applies to the Scheôl-passages in the *Psalms;* whether pre-Exilic or post-Exilic, they are in exact accordance with archaic and pre-Exilic thought. Men ' like sheep are laid in Scheôl ; Death is their shepherd . . . and their beauty shall the Under-world consume away ' (*Ps.* xlix. 14). But, according to early Euphratean belief, deliverance from this state. of things was possible in some cases. Thus, in Greek legend, Thêseus had been rescued from Hadês ; and, similarly, the Psalmist asserts, ' God will redeem my soul from the power of Scheôl (*Ib.* 15); whilst the pre-Exilic Hosea (xiii. 14) exclaims, ' I will ransom them from the power of Scheôl ; I will redeem them from death : O Death, where are thy plagues? O Scheôl, where is thy destruction?' The ' high goddess ' Persephoneia of the Homeric Nekyia, who is spoken of as the leading ruler of the Under-world, whilst Aïdôneus is entirely passed over, is a reduplication of the Ak. Ninkigal (' Queen-of-the-Great-place,' *i.e.,* the Under-world), the As. Allat, also called Ningê (' Queen-of-the-Under-world '), and whose husband is Mulgê (' King-of-the-Under-world '), identical with Mul-lil (Vide *sup.* p. 76).

XXII. Hekatê

We now approach a mysterious mythic personage whose origin is especially difficult to determine. It is easy to say at once, in accordance with general opinion, that Hekatê ('the Far-darting') is the rayed Moon, the moon being ever connected with triplicity; and that her phases of concept from grandeur and beauty down to horror and deformity, from the Hekatê of Hêsiod to the Hekatê of Shakspere, represent the splendour and dignity of the Night-queen combined with the horror of darkness as linked with evil dreams, ghosts and fiends. All this may be, and probably is, quite true so far as it goes; but a careful examination of the history of the goddess makes us doubt its sufficiency, as an exhaustive explanation of the myth. As to the name, many names purely Greek in form are either actually transliterations of non-Aryan names, or are put for them on account of similarity of sound. Thus, when a Phoenician Baal, appeased by human sacrifices, is called Meilichios ('the Gentle'), a euphemistic appellation, like Hekatê Meilionê, the Eumenides, Euxine, etc., such a title covers both the Greek word μείλικος, μειλίκιος and the Semitic word *melekh* ('king'). The name, therefore, is quite inconclusive. Much of the 'learning' respecting Hekatê has been carefully collected by Mr. Farnell (*Cults*, cap. xvi). As he notes, Steuding (in Roscher's *Lex. Hekate*) 'tacitly' accepts the view that she was (originally) 'a Hellenic divinity.' But, as he further observes, the goddess has 'no fixed and accepted genealogy'; and the famous passage about her in the *Theogony* is clearly an interpolation. 'It may be,' he says, 'that her cult invaded Greece, starting from the same land and following the same track as that of Dionysos.' In a word, he gives many excellent reasons in support of the view that the goddess is not in origin a Greek divinity; but hardly any evidence in favour of his own theory that she came to Hellas from the North. Of late the evidence in support of her non-Aryan origin has decidedly increased. M. Bérard (*Cultes Arcad.* p. 362) argues strongly in favour of a Semitic origin; observing, 'La comparaison entre Hécate et Baalat s'impose. Il serait étrange que deux peuples soient arrivés séparément à la même conception d'une triple déesse céleste, terrestre, infernale;' and proceeds to support his view by much interesting evidence. Amongst other points which may be urged in favour of a Semitic origin of the goddess are:—(1) Her position, as altogether distinct from the Zeus-family; (2) her participation in the Kabeiric cult of Samothrakê; (3) her connexion with horsemen and sailors; and (4) with Boiôtia and Boiôtian poets; (5) her triplicity; (6) her connexion with the Kretan Britomartis, Diktynna, the Net (δίκτυον)-goddess, Aphrodîtê of the Net (*Od.* viii), Eurynomê and Andromeda of the Chains, and whose Phoenician name Ast-No'emâ (= Gk. Astynomê) reappears in the Kretan translation as Britomartis ('the Sweet-virgin'), 'quod sermone nostro sonat virginem dulcem' (Solinus, xi. 8); (7) her titles Angelos, Eurippa, Sôteira and Kallistê; and (8) her connexion with Semelê, for 'alii χθονίαν Ἑκάτην, Boeotii Semelam credunt' (Macrob. I. xii. 23).

There is, however, yet another theory respecting the goddess, one which I formerly regarded as devoid of weight, but which, in the face of increasing evidence, I feel bound to present to the reader. Intercourse between Egypt and Phoenicia obtained from an exceedingly remote period; and there was a close connexion between the worship of the great Lower-Egypt-god Ptah or Phthah (the Memphic dialect form of the name) and the Pataikoi-cult of the Phoenicians. Ptah, the demiurge, 'the Artisan' (hence by Greeks called Hêphaistos), was often represented as a pigmy-figure, connected in idea with the embryo and similar to the dwarf Kabeiric figures with which the Phoenicians ornamented the prows of their war-galleys (Vide Hêrod. iii. 37). The Frog, called by the Graeco-Egyptian writer whom we know as Horapollôn, 'the representative of man in embryo,' was a symbol of Ptah; and on the wall of the temple at El-Khargeh, 'the ancient oasis of Ammon, in the Libyan desert,' were 'representations of the four elements divided into the male and female principle . . . represented snake-headed and frog-headed, holding their hands up in adoration' (Birch, in *Trans.* Soc. Bib. Archaeol. v. 295). One of these Diads is called *Hehu*, male, *Hehu-t*, female, the *t*, as in Semitic, marking the feminine termination. Iamblichos, when speaking of Ptah, also alludes to these eight powers (Cf. the seven Kabîrîm and Eschmûn, 'the Eighth'), 'four being male and four female' (*Peri Myst.* viii. 3); and in the Egyptian mythology we meet with the frog-headed goddess Heka, whom Birch (in Wilkinson's *Anct. Egyptians*, iii. 22) states 'symbolises the female principle of water.' In a popular story 'current at [the Egyptian] Thebes in the first years of the New Empire,' the goddess Hiquît or Heqit, 'the frog-goddess . . . one of the midwives who is present at the birth of the sun every morning,' is told to hasten with certain other goddesses to deliver a woman named Rudîtdidît of 'three children' (Vide Maspero, *Dawn of Civilization*, p. 388). Here we have a Heqit connected with triplicity; and Mr. F. Legge (*A Coptic Spell of the Second Century*, in *Proc*. Soc. Bib. Archaeol. May, 1897), apropos of the passage in the Incantation, 'Baubo, nourisher of oxen, nourisher of all things,' observes that 'in all the spells of the post-Christian Magic Papyri, Baubo [of Eleusinian fame] and Hecate are treated as the same person.' 'In the longer invocation from which it is apparently copied, Hecate is addressed as φρουνή or "she-toad."' He then refers to the 'Egyptian goddess Hek-t,' remarking, 'It is possibly she who was introduced into the Eleusinia under the name of Hecate. No really satisfactory etymology of the name Hecate has yet been given. If this be so, the patron goddess of sorcery . . . would seem to have had an Egyptian origin.'

Without pretending in this brief notice to solve so difficult a problem, I may add one or two further considerations. The equation Eg. Heqit = Gk. Hekatê is excellent, but this identification may perhaps not have been made until very late times; and of course it does not decide that the two were originally identical. The circumstance that neither Phoenicians nor Greeks possessed a frog-headed goddess is immaterial. Nothing but the intense philosophical symbolism of Egypt (by some confused with totemism) could have endured such a concept in concrete form. I know of no absolutely certain evidence of any direct archaic intercourse between Egypt and Hellas; but that Egyptian art had a considerable influence on that vanished civilization which we call Mykenaean is indisputable. Moreover, in Rhadamanthys (Vide *sup.* p. 132) we have, even in Homer, the undoubted figure of an Egyptian Sun-god. It is, on the whole, therefore, perfectly possible that the cult of Hekatê may have been originally Egyptian ; and may have reached Hellas through the Phoenicians. In this case she would naturally be more and more assimilated to such a goddess as the Semitic Baalâth; and the fact that her cult widely obtained on the coast of Asia Minor and in the islands of the Aigaion, is quite in harmony with this. In Greek belief Aiakos was associated with the Phoenician Minôs and the Egyptian Rhadamanthys in the High Commission of the Judges of the Under-world ; and Aiakos was the famous king of Aigîna ('the Goat'-island), a special possession of Poseidôn. 'And of all the divinities the Aiginêtans honour Hekatê the most, and celebrate her rites annually, saying that Orpheus the Thrakian introduced them [These baseless statements about an imaginary Orpheus have raised the idea that the Hecatê-ritual came from the North.]. Alkamenês [B.C. 440-400], as it seems to me, was the first who made the statue of Hekatê with three heads and three bodies ' (Paus. II. xxx. 2). Dogs were sacrificed to her (Vide Farnell, *Cults*, p. 597, for the various references), as to the Tyrian Hêraklês, Malekh-Bel, and to Melekhet - Artemis (Vide Movers, *Die Phönizier*, p. 404 *et seq.*) ; and she was even at times represented as dog-headed (Vide Hêsych. in voc. *Hekatês agalma*). I quite agree with Mr. Farnell that the belief of early Greece, as we know it, does not show us Hekatê in the lofty and varied position and character which is attributed to her by the author of the inserted passage, *Theogonia*, 409-52. But I do not doubt that this poet was far better acquainted with her archaic history than we can be ; and that he would not have ventured merely to draw on his imagination in the matter; especially when all had to be inserted in so famous and semi-sacred a work as the Greek *Book of the Generations*. There is one remarkable epithet applied to her which exactly agrees with the first appearance of Heqit in Egyptian myth as 'the Midwife.' Hekatê is 'from the beginning the Foster-mother' or 'Nursing-mother' (Κουροτρόφος) ; and, again, at Athens 'the Gene- tyllides, the divine midwives . . . were sometimes identified with Hekate' (Farnell, *Cults*, p. 519). She, says the poet, can increase the flocks and herds. It is not improbable that Kourotrophos was originally a translation of what Mr. Farnell calls 'the inexplic- able epithet Κελκαία,' which, applied to Artemis on account of her mythic resemblance to Hekatê, really belongs to the latter (Vide *Ib.* p. 518). The title, probably formed from the Sem. *kilkai-l*, 'to sustain,' 'nourish,' will thus mean 'the Nurturer.'

XXIII. Athênê Ilia

Reading the *Iliad* as a child, I used to think that the conduct of Athênê towards the Trojans, and her unrelenting hatred of them were very cruel, consider- ing the honour they paid her, and the efforts they made to appease her. In *Il.* vi. we read that on the direction of Helenos, 'far best of augurs', Hekabê and the Trojan women repaired to the temple of Athênê in the citadel and presented the goddess with a superb Sidonian *peplos*, which Theânô, the priestess, laid on the knees of her statue, and, at the same time prayed to her, in very touching words, to 'have mercy on the city and the little children. So spake she praying, but Pallas Athênê denied the prayer.' The poet evidently regards the Ilian, as identical with the Attic, Athênê; but such was not the case. The goddess in question was really the Phrygian Atê. Ilion was founded ἐπὶ τὸν λεγόμενον τῆς Φρυγίας Ἄτης λόφον (Apollod. III. xii. 3); and hence was called Ἄτης λόφος· οὕτως τὸ Ἴλιον ἐκαλεῖτο πρῶτον (Hêsych. *in voc.*). Ἄθας· θεός (Philôn Byb. ap. Stephanos Byzant. *in voc.* Λαοδίκεια). So, 'Ati appears in Atar-'ati = Gk. Atargatis (Antipatros of Tarsos, ap. Athenaios, viii. 8). (A)targatis = Derketô, and Antarata, a goddess of the Hittites. Prof. Sayce suggests that Atê 'was the female deity answering to the sun-god Atys or Attis'; and observes that the palladium of Troy was the 'meteoric stone' of the goddess, similar to the stone of the Hittite goddess of Ephesos, whom the Greeks called Artemis, and whose priestesses armed with the double-headed axe of Zeus Labrandeus ('Of-the-twy-headed axe', = Dionysos Pelekys), and with shield and bow, gave rise to the Greek Amazon-myth (Vide Sayce, *Herod.* p. 430; in *Trans.* Soc. Bib. Archaeol. vii. 260). He agrees that the confusion between Atê or Athê and Athê-nê merely arose from similarity of name. Here, then, is another instance of a non-Aryan Athênê. In *Gen.* xxxvi. 2 we read of 'Adâh the daughter of Elôn the ' Hitty,' *i.e.*, Hittite; and in *Gen.* iv. 19 a wife of Lâmech is so called. Semitically the name is explained as 'the Beauty.' Hêsychios gives Ἄδα· ὑπὸ Βαβυλωνίων ἡ Ἥρα, and Prof. Sayce quotes the

11

Apology of Melito to the effect that ' 'Ati was the
goddess of Adiabene, east of the Tigris.'   Her *peplos*
or sacred robe reminds us of that of Kharmôn-
Harmonia (Vide *sup*. p. 132), and of other Semitic
divinities, from whom it was ultimately adopted in
Athenian ritual.

Thus we see from such instances as Zeus Laphystios, Labrandeus, Lykaios, Meilichios ; Hêra Akraia;
Dêmêtêr Hippia, Melainê ; Athênê Ilia, Onka ;
Apollôn Ismênios, Karneios ; Artemis Braurônia,
Ephesia, Eurynomê, Kallistê, Limnâtis, Patrôa,
Kelkaia, Orthia, Taurikê ; and many other similar
cases,—for these are merely a few specimens,—how
constantly the Greeks bestowed the name of one of
their own Hellenic and Aryan divinities upon some
foreign god or goddess.   Until this principle is carefully and consistently taken into account, we shall
never arrive at a true understanding of Greek mythology as a whole.

XXIV. The Greek Constellation-myths

We must next consider the Hellenic mythology in
its connexion with the ancient constellation-figures,
by which I mean those described in the *Phainomena*
of Aratos.   And here, at the outset, I warn the
reader that the age of the Classicists, of whom
Otfried Müller was the greatest, and Robert Lowe,
Viscount Sherbroke, perhaps the last, has passed for
ever.   When Mr. Lowe, as Chancellor of the Ex-
chequer, was asked to give Government aid to
excavations at Troy, he glibly replied, 'Etiam periere
ruinae.'   People laughed, and said 'How smart' !
Then came the spade of Schliemann, and Mr. Lowe's
resuscitation of Latin ignorance seemed somewhat

silly. Sir G. C. Lewis was another famous member
of this school. His *Astronomy of the Ancients* is an
excellent compendium of Classical quotations, but
otherwise rather worse than worthless, *i.e.*, mischievous;
for, unfortunately for his fame, he lived long enough
to see and practically to reject the rapidly rising
sciences of Egyptology and Assyriology. About
these. Otfried Müller of course knew nothing ; and
his labours will ever merit the deepest respect.   It is
in no spirit of self-complacency that we speak of such
a man ; but, to quote a proverb which perchance may
be as old as the myth of the blinded Ôrîôn guided
by the dwarf Kedaliôn, who stands on his shoulders,
a subject treated in Phoenician art (Vide R. B. Jr.,
The Heavenly Display, Fig. xxxi. p. 39), ' A dwarf
on a giant's shoulders sees farther than the giant.'
The chief fault in the constellation studies of Müller
is a vast abuse of the argument from silence, which
should always be regarded with vigilant suspicion ;
and an entire failure to perceive that when we try to
explain the origin of any particular constellation-
figure by saying that someone unknown, thought that
certain stars resembled *e.g.*, an Arrow, and then
united them as a constellation called the *Arrow*,
which notion all the world accepted, *we are merely
inventing history, and practically only repeating that a
constellation called the Arrow exists.* Suppose this
theory were true in fact ; even then we could never
know that it was true.   In law a witness who swears
to facts which are true, but of which he is ignorant,
is liable to be proceeded against for perjury.   And
this illustration will show the grave impropriety of
representing hypotheses as facts.   If this theory of
the origin of the constellation-figures be further
tested by such an enquiry as, Why were these

11 *

particular stars considered to represent an arrow, and
not a sceptre or a spear ? no answer can be supplied.
On such lines the greatest ignoramus is on a par with
the deepest student. It is as easy for the former as
for the latter to suggest that someone thought that
certain stars resembled a ram in shape, and lo ! the
constellation *Aries* was formed. Let the reader look
at *Aries;* or, to take a constellation more frequently
visible, the well-known W of *Kassiepeia*, and he
will at once see that the stars of the one bear no
resemblance to a ram, nor the stars of the other to a
seated woman. Yet there was a reason for the
selection of these particular forms, a cause which can
only be discovered by careful research. I wish to
insist strongly on these principles; especially since
the history of the constellation-figures has been a
happy hunting-ground for ignorance and folly. Scores
of books have been published upon this subject, most
of them in English, replete with almost every possible
historical and philological absurdity; whilst remarkable for an entire ignorance respecting the real facts
of the case. It is, doubtless, difficult to overthrow
long established opinions, however baseless. But,
fortunately, errors do generally yield by degrees;
and if not formally renounced, are yet tacitly
abandoned. Let us remember, then, on the threshold
of the enquiry, that, in forming constellation-figures,
man has his meaning, his reason, his particular line
of thought; and was not merely influenced by an
arbitrary fancy. To give a fine illustration from
Prof. Ihering, quoted by Prof. Müller :—

' What could seem more magical than the auguria
taken by an army on its march ? Why did they
throw grain before the fowls and watch their move-

ments ? Because originally, as Prof. Ihering has
shown, when entering into an unknown country, it
was often a question of life and death whether the
grain and berries that were found growing wild were
poisonous or wholesome' (*C.* p. 460).

This fact was ascertained by means of domestic
fowls, the original purpose was forgotten, the ancient
practice was retained, and became 'magical.'

Nor, again, are we here concerned with savages,
and what they think and do, or may have thought
and done in archaic times. Strabo (XVI. ii. 24)
sums up the unhesitating opinion of antiquity, in his
dictum that 'astronomy and arithmetic came to the
Hellenes from the Phoenicians'; and all modern
research does but illustrate this cardinal historical
fact. He says that the Phoenicians were led,
naturally enough, to study these sciences from their
commercial accounts and sailings by night. In *The
Heavenly Display* I have shown at length that, in
Classical writers, the introducer or popularizer of
knowledge, is constantly described as its inventor.
Thus, according to Diogenês Laertios, Anaximandros
of Miletos, B.C. 610-547, 'was the first discoverer of
the gnomon'; whereas, as Hêrodotos (ii. 109) truly
says, ' The gnomon with the division of the day into
twelve parts, was received by the Hellenes from the
Babylonians.' The Greek constellation-myths are of
singular interest and importance, not merely because
they afford excellent studies in archaic psychology,
but also because they form an important link between
ourselves and that venerable Euphratean civilization
whence we have derived many of them, together with
our division of time into hours, minutes and seconds.

XXV. Palamêdês

Ere speaking of the constellation-figures and their attendant myths, we must notice the legend of a great semi-Greek hero always connected with them. The name of Nauplios (' Navigator ') is naturally attached to several personages in Greek mythico-historic legend ; two of whom are confounded together by Strabo (VIII. vi. 2), who also draws some erroneous conclusions founded on his own mistake. Nauplios, son of Poseidôn, reputed founder of Nauplia (Paus. II. xxxviii. 2), the port of Argos, and called by some the originator of the constellation *Ursa Maj.* (Theôn, in Arat. *Phainom.* 27), is a representative of Phoenician knowledge and colonization. Another Nauplios, a similar personage, is styled king of Euboia and sire of Palamêdês, of whom he is thus made to speak in a Fragment of the *Nauplios* of Sophoklês, which fortunately has been preserved :—

Οὗτος δ'ἐφεῦρε τεῖχος 'Αργείων στρατῷ
σταθμῶν, 'αριθμῶν καὶ μέτρων εὑρήματα·
κ'ακεῖν' ἔτευξε πρῶτος ἐξ ἑνὸς δέκα,
κἀκ τῶνδέ γ'αὖθις εὗρε πεντεκοντάδας
ἐις χίλι· οὗτος εἰς στρατῷ φρυκτωρίαν
ὕπνου φυλάξεις, ἔς θ'ἕω σημάντρια
ἐδειξε κ'νέφηνεν οὐ δεδειγμένα·
ἐφεῦρε δ'ἄστρων μέτρα καὶ περιστροφὰς·
τάξεις τε ταύτας, οὐράνιά τε σήματα,
ναῶν τε ποιμαντῆρσιν ἐνθαλασσίων
Ἄρκτου στροφάς τε καὶ Κυνὸς ψυχρὰν δύσιν.

Here, in accordance with the statement of Strabo (*sup.* p. 165), we find the arts of fortification, in which the Phoenicians excelled; of numbers and arithmetic, of military watch and ward, of navigation, and of astronomy, including the dividing of the stars into constellational groups and the naming of such groups, ascribed to Palamêdês, a grandson of the Phoenician Poseidôn (Eurip. *Iph. en. Aul.* 198). Homer is silent concerning the hero ; and for this two reasons at once present themselves, (1) the death of Palamêdês occurred prior to the opening of the *Iliad;* and (2) the poet 'sang for the glory of Greece' (Gladstone, *Juv. Mun.* p. 145). Palamêdês, a personage in many points superior to the Hellenic heroes, and, according to legend, infamously treated by them, and particularly by the poet's favourite Odysseus (Vide Hyginus, *Fab.* cv; Paus. X. xxxi. 1), would naturally be somewhat avoided by a very patriotic Hellene. Like his sire Nauplios, Palamêdês, as a representative of the historical Phoenician element in Hellas, is in almost constant collision with the Greek element, by which he is eventually overcome. But, although Homer ignores him, Polygnôtos, a native of that Thasos which was so long a famous Phoenician colony, did not. In his mighty picture of the Under-world, perhaps the finest painting ever executed, and which adorned the Leschê at Delphoi (For a detailed account of it, vide R. B. Jr., *Tellis and Kleobeia*), the Thasian master represented Palamêdês playing at dice, a sport which he was said to have invented (Paus. II. xx. 3), with Salaminian Aias and Thersîtês (*Ibid.* X. xxxi. 1). And who and what is Palamêdês but the Phoenician Baal-Middoh ('Lord-of-the-Measure;' cf. Palaimôn = Baal-Hamon; Bellerophôn = Baal-Raphon, 'le dieu de la sante.' Bérard.), god of numbers, figures, weights, scales, dice, letters, arithmetic, astronomy; and the latter part of whose name was understood as meaning 'the Wise' (Cf. Mêdeia, 'the Wise'-woman). In Greek legend he is

particularly connected with the invention of the letters
θ, φ, χ, and ξ (Vide Canon Is. Taylor, *The Alphabet*,
ii. 70). Another somewhat similar personage is
Agamêdês (= Sem. ' The Great-measurer,' Gk. ' The
Very-wise '), who represents Phoenician constructive
ability in Boiôtia, and who forms with Trophônios
(= Ph. Baal Trophâ, ' the Lord of Cure.'   Bérard.),
the Diad of god and god-introducer.

In the last line of the passage from the *Nauplios*,
Sophoklês sums up the astronomical aspect of the
matter, by naming the *Bear*, as protagonist of the
northern, and the *Dog* on behalf of the southern,
constellations; and it will be observed that he speaks
not of *Seïrios*, generally merely the Dog-star, but of
Kuôn, the constellation, whose *frigidum occasum* on the
seventh day of *Sagittarius*, accompanied by tempest,
had already been noted by the Athenian astronomer
Euktêmôn (Vide Geminos, *Eisagôgê eis ta Phainom.*
Cap. xvi. Calendar), who about B.C. 432, together
with Metôn, introduced the famous cycle of nineteen
years, the ἐννεακαίδεκα κύκλα φαεινοῦ ἠελίοιο (Aratos,
Diosêmeia, 21), which had long before been known
to the Babylonians.

XXVI. The Ancient Greek Constellation-figures

The ancient Greek Constellation-figures, as given
by Aratos, are :—

I. Northern Signs. These group themselves
thus :—

1. The *Bears* and *Bearward* (Vide *sup.* p. 65).
As Achilles Tatius (*Eisagôgê*, xxxix) truly says, the
Bears, *Serpent*, and *Kêpheus* were not in the

Chaldaean sphere. In this the seven stars of the *Great Bear* were called (Sum.-Ak.) *Margidda* ('the Long-chariot'), which 'all the year is fixed' (*kal satti izzaz, W.A.I.* III. lii. No. 1, Rev. l. 24), *i.e.*, around the pole. And this simple astronomical dictum is expressed, or possibly even translated, by Homer, when he says that it 'turns round without moving away' (*Il.* xviii. 488). Thus, the Phrygians called it Κίκλην ('the Circler.' Hêsych. *in voc.*). The *Bear* was the Mediterranean, the *Wain* the Euphratean, name of the constellation. Hence the two names in Homer.

2. The Family-group. *Kêpheus* (Vide *sup.* p. 141), *Kassiepeia* (= Kallonê, 'the Beauty,' Souidas, *in voc.* Ph. Qassiu-peaêr.), Andromeda (Vide *sup.* p. 141) and Perseus (Vide *sup.* p. 141). 'The Greeks know that Perseus was the founder of Mykênai' (Paus. II. xv. 4), = Ph. Makhâneh ('the Camp.' Bérard. Cf. Mêkônê, Mukônê, Migônion, etc.). The (southern) *Whale* is a detached member of this group. These constellations are Phoenician in origin.

3. The *Kneeler* (= *Hêraklês*), constellationally connected (1) with the *Serpent*, the **Ph.** *Nâkhâsch qadmûn* ('Old-serpent'), the γέρων Ὀφίων of the kosmogony of the Phoenician-sprung Pherekydês of Syros; and (2) with the *Arrow* and the three Birds, the *Vulture* (the *Lyre*), the *Bird* (otherwise the *Swan*), and the *Eagle*. This group and myth is Euphratean. Merôdach-Gilgames (the Gilgamos of Aelian, xii. 21) wars against the three Demon-birds; Gilgames in Euphratean art is pre-eminently the Kneeler, and, hence, in Western Hellas the constellation is known as *Engonasin*, whence the Lat.

Nixus (Cicero), *Genunixus* (Ovid, Germanicus), 'Nixa genu species' (Manilius), *Ingeniculatus* (Vitruvius), *Ingeniculus* (Firmicus). This special attitude links Hêraklês, the Kneeler, with Euphratean art of the most archaic types and times : witness the specimen from Nippur given by Hilprecht, *The Babylonian Expedition of the University of Pennsylvania*, 1896, Vol. i. Pt. ii. Pl. xxvi : ' Man fighting a lion.' The Babylonian cylinders show the kneeling Gilgames in conflict with a lion, and the type continues from age to age, until we come to the fine kneeling Phoenician Hêraklês of Thasos (Figured by Svoronos, *Sur la Signification des Types Monétaires des Anciens*, 1894, Pl. xvi).

In Eastern Hellas the *Kneeler* continued to be known as *Hêraklês*. Peisandros of Kameiros, cir. B.C. 650, was author of the *Hêrakleia*, in which it is said that the hero was first represented with club and lion's skin, and his special labours fixed at twelve in number. There is no invention in all this ; Peisandros merely faithfully portrayed Gilgames-Hêraklês, the Sun-god, who has a special labour in each month and Sign of the Zodiac ; and Peisandros himself merely copied from Pisînos of Lindos, as he in turn received these stories from his predecessors. The successor of Peisandros was Panyasis of Halikarnassos, put to death cir. B.C. 457, who also wrote or re-edited a *Hêrakleia*, in fourteen books containing 9000 lines, and who called the *Kneeler Hêraklês* (Vide Avienus, *Aratea*, 175).

4. The *Charioteer* (Poseidôn), with his special animals the *Horse* and *Dolphin*, placed side by side.

5. The *Crown* of Dionysos. ' Emere ac vendere instituit Liber Pater. Idem diadema, regium insigne,

et triumphum invenit' (Pliny, *Hist. Nat.* vii. 57);
that is to say, the Sun-god established civilization,
and first triumphantly crowned heaven with his
glowing circle. Ariadnê ('the Very-holy'), daughter
of Minôs, to whom this *Crown* was given, probably
= Ph. Areth (Vide Bunsen, *Egypt's Place*, iv. 246).

6. *The Snake-holder.* = the Ph. Eschmûn, 'a
native Phoenician god,' as Damaskios (*Isidórou Bios,*
ccxlii) calls him, Aish-qel ('the Lively-fire'), a god
of healing, called by the Greeks Êpios ('the
Kindly'). Aishqel-Êpios = Gk. Asklêpios, Lat.
Aesculapius, Aescolapeius, ultimately incorporated
into the family of Greek divinities as a son of
Apollôn ; figured as a Snake-holder on the Phoenician coins of Kossura, and, with his sacred serpents,
specially revered at Epidauros.

7. *Deltôton.* = The (isosceles) *Triangle,* placed
with the Family-group of Phoenician divinities;
and an exact celestial reproduction of the sacred
pyramidal monoliths, specimens of which still exist
in Kypros, and appear on her coinage. It further
serves as a symbol of that revered form the Tripod.

Such are the nineteen ancient Northern Signs.

II. *Central Signs.* Composed of :—

1. The twelve Signs of the Zodiac, known in the
Euphrates Valley from a remote antiquity. As
Prof. Sayce observes, the *Virgin* = Istar-'Asch-
thârth-Astartê, called Astartê Erek-hayim (= Gk.
Erykînê, Êrigonê, Herkyna, etc.), *i.e., Longae vitae
auctor* (Vide Bérard, *Cultes Arcad.* p. 148 ; R. B. Jr.,
The Zodiacal Virgo, 1886). The idea of a goddess
at the same time virgin and mother is very archaic
(Cf. Paus. II. xxxvii. 2).

2. The *Clusterers* (= *Pleiades*), subsequently called by play on words ' Doves ' and ' Sailing '-stars, often represented on coins by a Grape-cluster.

Early coins of Phaistos in Krêtê show *Hêraklês* with *Lion*-skin, at his foot *Crab*, striking at *Hydra*. This group forms an interesting illustration of the constellational position of *Cancer*, *Leo*, and *Hydra*.

III. *Southern Signs.* These group themselves thus:—

1. *Ôríôn*, his *Dogs* and the *Hare*, a type of the sun-chased Moon. (For instances of the Hare-moon type, vide Gubernatis, *Zoological Mythology*, ii. 76 ; Sebillót, *Traditions de la Haute Bretagne;* Schlie- mann, *Troy and its Remains*, p. 136 ; Lajard, *Culte de Mithra*, Pl. lii. 6). The origin of this myth is Euphratean ; Marduk (Marûdûku probably = the Ak, Uru-dug ; ' Benefactor of man ') the solar hero, is attended by his ' four divine dogs,' Ukkumu (' Despoiler '), Akkulu (' Devourer '), Iksuda (' Cap- turer '), and Iltebu (' Carrier-away '). The number is not accidental, but represents the flow of light from the Diurnal-sun to the four quarters.

The gigantic (Cf. Pindar, *Isth.* iii. 67 : φύσιν 'Ωαριωνείαν. Sun as huge compared with stars.) Uríôn, Aoríôn, Ôaríôn, Ôríôn (= Sem. Ury, ' the Fiery-one,' a well known proper name, + *ôn*. ' The formation of proper names of men and places by the termination *ón* is excessively common.' Steinthal. Cf. Dâg-ôn, Shimsh-ôn.), who, in Phoenician Boiô- tia, which claimed to be his birthplace, was also called Kandaôn (Tzetzês, in Lykophrôn, 328), = Sem. Kohain-dayan (' The Prince-the-Judge '), is a variant phase of the solar Dionysos. The blinded Ôriôn (= the solar eye quenched at night) recovers his sight by journeying through the Under-world, guided by the Kabeiric dwarf Kedaliôn (= 'One in charge'—of the dead) = Seirios, leader and brightest of the stars, to the East (= the reappearance of the solar eye next day). Naturally Ôriôn is loved by Êôs (the Dawn), and, gigantic though he be, he is slain by Artemis (the Lunar-power, *Od.* v. 121-4) by means of a still huger Scorpion (= Darkness. Vide *inf.* p. 177). He dies in Paustêria (the 'Death' mountain), in the West (Hêsych. in voc. *Paustêria*). Goodliest of men (*Od.* xi. 310), the Boiôtian poetess Korinna represented him as a noble and pious civilizer of a barbarous country, a frequent rôle of the Sun-god; and he is reduplicated in the brightest of constellations (For detailed consideration of the Ôriôn-myth, vide R. B. Jr., *The Great Dionysiak Myth*, ii. 270 *et seq.; Eridanus*, sec. iv; *The Myth of Kirkê*, p. 146 *et seq.*). The *Dog* is shown on a Euphratean Boundary Stone (Vide R. B. Jr., *The Heavenly Display*, Fig. lxi., p. 78) in precisely the same attitude as on a modern star-map.

The *Lesser Dog, Prokyôn* ('the Dog's-precursor'), whose rising announced the coming of *Sirius*, is but a single star, not a constellation, in Aratos. *Prokyôn* appears in an interesting legend which illutrates the introduction of the Semitic constellation-figures into Hellas. Dionysos, on arriving at Attikê, was hospit-ably received by Ikarios, to whom he gave the vine. Some peasants who became intoxicated, thinking they were poisoned, murdered Ikarios and buried his body, which was at length found by his daughter Êrigonê, who was conducted to the grave by his faithful little dog Maira ('the Sparkler'). Êrigonê, from grief, hung herself on the tree beneath which he was buried. The god then punished the Athenians with madness, in which condition the Athenian maidens hung themselves. At length Dionysos, Ikarios, and Êrigonê were propitiated by the institution of the Festival of the Aiôra ('Suspension in air,' Swinging); and Ikarios was translated to the skies as *Boôtés*, Êrigonê as *Virgo*, and Maira as *Prokyôn*. The legend furnishes one of many instances of opposition to the introduction of the Dionysiac ritual. Similar circum· stances are described as occurring in Argolis, and two familiar instances are those of Lykourgos (*Il.* vi. 130-40) and Pentheus (Eurip. *Bakchai*). Ikaros or Ikarios is identical with the Megarian hero Kar the Karian, who is said to have built the Akropolis of Megara, where were temples of Dionysos and Aphrodîtê and a statue of Asklêpios-Eschmûn (Paus. I. xl. 4). The underlying historical fact is that the Karians were constantly employed by the Phoenicians as mercenaries. I noticed (*Sup.* p. 171) that Êrigonê = Sem. Erek-hayim ; and the circumstance that Êrigonê and Êrigoneia ('the Early-born') were independent Greek names for the Dawn, merely facilitated the transliteration. The star *a Canis Minoris* is called by the Arabs *Ghomaïsâ* ('The Watery-eyed'), a reminiscence how, in the myth, the 'canis ululans Merâ' (Hyginus, *Fab.* cxxx) wept for the death of its master. The supposed fate of Êrigonê and the ritual of the Aiôra are connected with the cult of the goddess of the net and chains (Vide p. 156).

2. The *Stream.* = the Euphrates (Vide R. B. Jr., *Eridanus, River and Constellation*).

3. The *Sea-monster.* Belongs to the Phoenician

Family group, and is a reduplication of the Euphratean Tiâmat, Heb. Tehôm ('the Deep'), the Thanatth of Bêrôsos ; the Tauthê of Damaskios, and called in the inscriptions 'the Dragon of the Sea.'

4. The *Southern Fish.* A reduplication of the zodiacal *Fishes*, themselves originally one, a second *Fish* having been added for the double or intercalary month Ve-Adar. All this watery part of the heavens, into which falls the stream of Êridanos, and which is occupied by the *Sea-monster*, the three *Fish*, the *Sea-goat*, the *Water-pourer*, the *Dolphin*, and the *Sea-horse* (Pêgasos), who is represented as just emerging out of it, was 'the region of Êa' (Poseidôn), in Euphratean parlance.

5. The *Altar.* A reduplication of the *Holy-altar*, the original seventh Sign of the Zodiac, superseded by the *Claws* of the *Scorpion*, which embraced it, and which in turn gave way to the Egyptian Sign of the *Balance.* Τὰς Χηλὰς, τὰς καλουμένας ὑπ' Αἰγυπτίων Ζυγὸν (Achilles Tatius), = *Libra.*

6. The *Centaur.* A reduplication of *Sagittarius.* On a West Asian Gem (figured by me in *Euphratean Stellar Researches*, Pt. iv. p. 4) the *Centaur* and *Wild-beast* (afterwards called *Lupus*) appear exactly as Cheirôn ('the Handy' = skilful) is depicted on the famous and archaic Chest of Kypselos (Vide Paus. V. xix. 2).

7. The *Water-snake*, with the *Bowl* and *Crow.* The contest of Hêraklês and the Hydra is a reduplication of the Euphratean myth of the fight between Marduk and Tiâmat, the Dragon of chaos, darkness, and evil, further reduplicated in the *Sea-monster*. 'The monstrous snake' with its 'seven heads,' 'the strong serpent of the sea' (*W.A.I.* II. xix. No. 2, ll.

7, 8), is a familiar figure in Euphratean myth. She was the mother of a terrible brood, including man-headed birds, raven-headed men, etc., representing storm, tempest, etc. (For some myths connected with the *Bowl*, vide *Eridanus*, p. 19).

8. The *Ship*. Called by the Greeks *Argô* ('the Bright'). The great solar voyage across heaven is an idea equally common to Akkadian, Semite, Egyptian and Aryan. Mythic examples of it are the voyage of Gilgames, who had a special 'ship' or 'ark'; the voyage of Melqârth to the West; Apollôn Delphinios ; Hêlios and Hêraklês and the solar boat-cup ; the voyage of Râ and his crew in the solar barque; and, I may add, Arthur in the barge. That there was also an actual British chieftain around whom masses of solar myth clustered, I quite believe.

XXVII. The Signs of the Zodiac

I. *Origin.* The Signs of the Zodiac were not the product of idle fancy or arbitrary invention; nor, again, did they originate from a real or supposed resemblance between their forms and the actual configuration of the stars, although in several instances, *e.g.*, the *Bull* and the *Scorpion*, the actual configuration was utilized in the expression of a pre-existing concept. The Signs were, in truth, reduplications of simpler ideas connected with natural phenomena. For centuries astrologers, without knowing why, have termed them alternately 'diurnal' and 'nocturnal'; and this is quite correct, inasmuch as they were in origin simply symbolical representations, of a kind very familiar to the mythological imagination, of certain ordinary diurnal and nocturnal phenomena. They belong to a class of ideas which arose naturally and spontaneously in the archaic mind, those anthropomorphic and animal similes and comparisons which occur equally in the Akkadian *Hymns*, the Egyptian *Book of the Dead*, or the *Rig-Veda*. On careful analysis the origin of the Twelve Signs appears thus :—

I.   Diurnal Signs.

1. The Ram-sun, afterwards reduplicated as *Aries*.

2. Sun and Moon, afterwards reduplicated as *Gemini*.

3. The Lion-sun, afterwards reduplicated as *Leo*.

4. The Daily-sacrificed Sun, afterwards reduplicated as *Ara*.

5. The Archer-sun, afterwards reduplicated as *Sagittarius*.

6. The Rain-giving Sun, afterwards reduplicated as *Aquarius*.

II.   Nocturnal Signs.

1. The Moon-bull, afterwards reduplicated as *Taurus*.

2. Darkness, afterwards reduplicated as *Cancer*.

3. The Moon-goddess (afterwards Evening-star), afterwards reduplicated as *Virgo*.

4. Darkness, afterwards reduplicated as *Scorpio*.

5. The Sea-sun, afterwards reduplicated as *Capricornus*.

6. The Nocturnal-sun, afterwards reduplicated as *Piscis*.

12

II. *The Gilgames Epic.* The archaic Euphratean story of the solar hero Gilgames described a fresh labour and adventure in each Sign and month, and thus formed the prototype of the Hêraklês-myth. From such fragments of the Tablets as remain we can reconstruct the principal incidents as follows:—

1. *Ram.* Birth, parentage, etc., of Gilgames.

2. *Bull.* Account of the mysterious, horned Êabani ('Êa-made-me').

3. *Twins.* Gilgames and Êabani.

4. *Crab.* Overthrow of the tyrant Khumbaba (Cf. the name Κομβάβος Lucian, *Peri tês Sy. Thê.* xix).

5. *Lion.* The slaughter of the Lion.

6. *Virgin.* The Adventures of Istar.

7. *Altar and Claws.* The descent to the Underworld.

8. *Scorpion.* The Death of Êabani, and sickness of Gilgames.

9. *Archer.* The Scorpion-men and the Bright Grove.

10. *Sea-Goat.* The Voyage of Gilgames.

11. *Water-pourer.* The Story of the Deluge.

12. *Fish.* The Mourning for Êabani, the Rising of his Ghost, etc.

Most of these instances are reproduced or appear in variant phases of the subsequent myths of the solar hero. Êabani, the wise Man-beast, is reduplicated in the good and wise Centaur-Cheirôn.

III. *The Sumero-Akkadian months.* These, the first of which corresponded with our March-April, were called :—

1. *Bara Ziggar*, = ' The Upright Altar ' = (ab-

breviated form) 'The Altar,' or 'The Sacrifice,' *i.e.*, of the Golden-ram-sun, offered daily ; basis of the Phoenician ritual sacrifice of an only son, and of the myth of the death of Tammuz, 'the Only-son' (Vide *sup.* p. 148). So, in the Phoenician myth, Êl-Kronos 'had an only son who was on that account called Iedoud (= Yehûd, Heb. Yâhid, 'the Only-begotten'). When the country was placed in jeopardy during a great war, he decked his son in royal apparel, erected an altar, and sacrificed him thereon' (*Frag.* ex Philonis *De Judaeis* Libro).

2. *Gut-sidi*, = 'the Directing Bull,' = 'the Bull,' as, prior to B.C. 2540, the leading Sign.

3. *Mun-ga*, = 'the Making of Bricks,' = 'the Brick,' or 'the Twins.' The archaic kosmogonic myth or legend attached to the month, is that of the Two Brethren, often hostile, and the Building of the First City. Sun and Moon, constellationally reduplicated in the two stars called by the Greeks *Kastor* and *Polydeukês*, after the Aryan Diad of the Asvinau-Dioskouroi.

4. *Su-kulna*, = 'The Seizer-of-seed,' = 'the Boon' (of Seed).

5. *Ne-ne-gar*, = 'Fire-making-fire' 'the Fire,' *i.e.*, the fiery *Leo*.

6. *Ki-Gingir-na*, = 'The Errand of Istar,' = 'the Errand.'

7. *Tul-ku*, = 'The Holy Altar,' = 'the Altar.'

8. *Apin-dúa*, = 'Opposite to the Foundation,' = 'the Foundation.'

9. *Gan-ganna*, = 'the Very-cloudy,' = 'the Cloud.'

10. *Abba-e*, = 'The Case-of-the-Rising' (of the Sun), = 'the Cave.'

12 *

11. *As-a-an,* = ' The Curse-of-rain,' = ' the Curse,' or ' the Rainy.'

12. *Se-kisil,* = ' The Sowing of Seed ' = ' Seed.'

IV. *The Sumero-Akkadian Names of the Signs.*

1. *Lu-lim* (' The Ram '). Also called *Ku-e,* = As. *Aggâru* (' the Messenger ').

2. *Gut-anna* (' The Bull-of-heaven ').

3. *Mastabba-galgal* (' The Great-twins ').

4. *Nagar-asurra* (' The Workman-of-the-River-bed '), = the *Crab.*

5. *Lik-makh* (' The Great-dog '), = the *Lion.*

6. *Ab-nam* (' The Proclaimer-of-rain ').

7. *Bir* (' The Light '), = the *Altar,* lighted.

8. *Gir-anna* (' The Scorpion-of-heaven '), commonly called *Girtab* (' Scorpion,' lit. ' Seizer-and-stinger.').

9. *Papilsak* (' Winged-fire-head '), = the *Archer.*

10. *Muna-kha* (' The Goat-fish '), = *Capricorn.*

11. *Gu-la* (' The Urn '—of the *Waterpourer*).

12. *Dur-ki* (' The Place of the Cord '). Which binds the *Fishes.*

V. *The Babylonio-Assyrian Names of the Signs.*

1. *Kusarikku* (' The Ram ').

2. *Alpu* (' The Bull ').

3. *Tuâmu rabûti* (' The Great-twins ').

4. *Pulukku* (' The Division '), *i.e.,* the ' Colure ' (Gk. *kolouros*), the great circle passing through the solstitial points. Practically this = the *Crab,* perhaps called *Sertânu.*

5. *Arû* (' The Lion ').

6. *Sîru* (' The Ear-of-corn). *Spica* (*a Virginis*).

7. *Zibânîtu* ('The Claws'). These held the circular *Altar* (Vide R. B. Jr., *Remarks on the Euphratean Astronomical Names of the Signs of the Zodiac*, Sec. vii. Figs. 12-14).

8. *Aqrabu* ('The Scorpion').

9. *Qastu* ('The Bow').

10. *Sahu* ('The Ibex').

11. *Kâ* ('The Urn'), Ph. and Heb. *ka-d*, whence Gk. κάδος.

11. *Nunu* ('The Fishes'). The Ak *dur* = Bab.-As. *riksu*, 'cord,' and the *Riksu-Nuni* ('Cord of the Fishes') is 'the tail-connecting link' of Aratos (*Phainom.* 245), the star *a Piscium*, called *Nodus* in Cicero's Aratos, and now known as *Okda* (Arab. *Uqdat*, 'The Knot'), and *Rischa*, a corrupt Arabic form of the As. *riksu*.

In the Graeco-Babylonian period, subsequent to Alexander, the Signs are technically known as:—

1. *Ku.* = *Kusarikku* ('Ram').

2. *Te or Te-te.* = Ak. *dimmena*, As. *timmenu*, 'foundation-stone,' 'foundation.' The reference is to *Taurus* as originally the first of the Signs. *Timmenu* is abraded to *tim, tem, te.* The two starting-points (*Te + Te*) are the *Bull* and the *Cluster*, = the Pleiad.

3. *Mas* or *Mas-mas* = *Mastabba-galgal*.

4. *Khas* ('The Division'). Vide *sup.* *Pulukku*.

5. *A.* = *Arû* ('Lion').

6. *Ki.* = *Sîru* ('Ear-of-corn').

7. *Bir.* = 'The Light' (Vide *sup.* p. 180).

8. *Gir.* = *Girtab* ('Scorpion').

9. *Pa.* = Papilsak (Vide *sup.* p. 180).

10. *Sah.* = *Sahu* ('Ibex').

11. *Gu.* = *Gula* ('Urn').

12. *Zib* (' The Boundary '), *i.e.*, the end of the Signs.

VI. *The Phoenician Names of the Signs.* Philôn of Byblos translated the work of Sanchouniathôn *On the Phoenician Letters*, and, in a passage on the nature of the Serpent, preserved in Eusebios (*Prop. Euan.* i. 10), he says, Εἴρηται δὲ ἡμῖν περὶ αὐτοῦ ἐν τοῖς ἐπιγραφομένοις περὶ Ἐθωθιῶν. As Lenormant observes, ' Les 'εθώθια sont manifestement les signes célestes, *êthûth*, hébr. *ôthôth* ' (*Les Origines*, i. 552). The Phoenician treatises on the constellation-figures are unfortunately lost ; but patient research will enable us to reconstruct the Phoenician sphere. The Signs were :

1. *Teleh* (' The Lamb '). A word applied to any young creature (Cf. Aramaic *Talitha*).
2. Aleph (' The Bull ' or Bull's head '). So Hêsychios : Ἄλφα· βοὸς κεφαλή. Φοίνικες.
3. *Thomîm* (' The Twins ').
4. *Sertân* (' The Crab ').
5. *Layish*. (' The Lion '). Whence the Kretan Λίς (Hêsychios).
6. *'Aschthârth* (Astartê), and perhaps *Bethûlûh* (' Virgin ').
7. *Perosûth?* (' Claws ').
8. *Aqrab* (' The Scorpion ').
9. *Qesheth* (' The Bow ').
10. *Gedy* (' The Kid ').
11. *Dely* (' The Bucket ').
12. *Dagîm* (' The Fishes ').

The *Pleiades* are named Heb. and Ph. *Kîmah*, Bab. *Kimtu* (' the Family '). The Signs collectively are called Sum.-Ak. *Innun* ('the Watches'), Bab.-As. *Mazârâti*, Heb.-Ph. *Mazzârôth*, LXX. Μαζουρὼθ, the night-watches being marked by the transit of the constellations.

VII. *The Signs in India.* After the age of Alexander the Hindûs became acquainted with the Signs. The Greek forms *Krios, Tauros, Didymoi, Kolouros* (Vide *sup.* p. 180), *Leôn, Parthenos, Zugon* ('the Yoke'), *Skorpios, Toxotês, Aiyokerôs, Hydrochoös,* and *Ichthyes,* reappear in Hindu astronomy as *Kriya, Tâvurî, Jituma, Kulîra, Leya, Pâthona, Jûka, Kaurpya, Taukshika, Akokera, Hridroqa,* and *Ittha.* Similarly, the planets *Hermês, Arês, Kronos, Zeus,* and *Aphrodîtê,* reappear as *Himna, Âra, Koṇa, Jyau,* and *Asphujit, Hêlios* becoming *Heli.* The extrazodiacal constellations reappear in the same way, *e.g., Kassiepeia* becomes *Kasyapi, Andromeda, Antarmada,* etc. When the Sk. forms of these names were first met with, it was (not altogether unnaturally) supposed that India had possessed the Signs from time immemorial, and had bestowed them on the West.

VIII. *The Signs in Egypt.* The Greeks also introduced the Signs into Egypt, where they appear in the well-known Zodiacs of Esneh and Denderah, etc., which were formerly supposed to be of an immense antiquity.

The notion, at one time prevalent, that the Signs were only introduced into Hellas at a comparatively late period, is as baseless as the theory that Alexandrian grammarians and poets tacked astronomical myths on to this or that personage at their own sweet will. Such plodding souls as the author of the *Katasterismoi*, Hyginus and others never dreamed of taking any liberties of the kind; but they had before them numerous authors now unfortunately lost, and the loss of this mass of evidence has made these delusions possible. Had we only the works of such writers as Peisandros, Pisînos, Panyasis, Aga-osthenês of Naxos, whose history of that island was used by Aratos, etc., the task of tracing the history of the introduction of the Signs into Hellas would have been far easier. But, whilst refined common sense will assure us that the Phoenician sailors would bring their lore with them as well as their letters, we are not left to this inference, certain as it is. We find archaic Sign-myths connected with Phoenician personages. The *Ram* with Athamas; the *Bull*, *Crab*, *Hydra*, *Lion*, Love-goddess (*Virgin*), etc., with Hêraklês; the *Scorpiôn* with Ôrîôn, the *Goats* (*Aix* and *Aigokerôs*) with Krêtê; the *Fishes* with Derketô, and thus on. *Aix* (= *Capella*, *a* Aurigae) is called ᾿Αμαλθεία, = Sem. L'Ammâ-θεία ('To the Divine-mother'), and the 'Olenian' Goat, because carried on the 'arm' (ὠλένη, *ulna*), as indeed it appears in countless instances on the Monuments of Babylonia. But, without further enlarging upon these matters here, I trust that the foregoing brief presentation of facts, many of which are by no means readily accessible, will enable the reader to grasp clearly the general historical progress of the Signs of the Zodiac.

XXVIII. The Homeric Constellations

'Homer, who is most accurate in everything' (Athen. v. 6), refers by name to the *Bear*, *Plough-man*, *Clusterers*, *Rainy-ones* (*Hyades*), *Dog*, and

Óríŏn. He refers generally to ' all the Signs (τείρεα)
with which the heaven is crowned.' The suggestions that this line is spurious, are baseless. He
also observes that the *Bear* alone (*i.e.*, of those constellations which he mentions) does not dip in ocean.
Strabo, stumbling very needlessly over this simple
statement, understands Homer to assert that the *Bear*
was the only constellation in the sky which does
not dip. If a great man makes a mistake, he is
generally eagerly followed; and so all the world have
blindly accepted Strabo's blunder. Homer is not
writing a *Phainomena;* he names the *Bear*, as head
of the northern Signs ; *Óríŏn*, as head of the
southern ; and Pleiads and Hyads, as representing
the Zodiac. Incidentally he refers to the *Dog* and
to *Boótês*, 'that setteth after a long time,' or 'at
length' (*Od.* v. 272). This latter invaluable reference shows that Homer alluded to the constellation
as it is mapped at present ; he was not referring to
the star *Arktouros* (Vide Lewis, *Astron. of the
Ancts.* p. 59 ; W. W. Merry, *Odyssey*, i. 282). This
also was quite understood by the ancients (Vide
Aratos, *Phainom.* 579-85, and Schol.) ; and, like
other Homeric statements, was carefully imitated
down to the end of the Classical period. The
supporters of the argument from silence, those who
hold that Homer did not know of this or that
Aratean constellation, have never really thought out
the matter. Anyone who had once marked on the
sky as groups the seven *Wain*-stars, *Boótês*, Pleiads,
Hyads, and *Óríŏn*, would not stop there ; he would
form other combinations also. The only one of the
five planets named by Homer is *Hesper-Phospher.*
Will it be contended that he was ignorant of the

other four ? If there can be anyone who thinks so, let him re-read that superb description of the cloudless starry heaven which closes *Il.* viii., and of which Tennyson has given such a matchless rendering, a night when ' the immeasurable heavens break open to their highest,' and when ' all stars are seen ' ; and then let him recant so grievous a heresy. But, if the bard, whilst well wotting *Jupiter*, or *Mars*, or *Saturn*, did not choose to name them, although he might readily have done so, is it strange that he is silent concerning the *Ram* and his fellows, when there was no reason in the story to refer to them ? Mark the account of Odysseus sailing by night,—for stars are sent by Zeus as portents for mariners (*Il.* iv. 75-6), a thoroughly Phoenician opinion,— how he views Pleiads, *Ploughman*, and *Bear*, keeping the latter on his left (for Greek-like, he steered by the *Great Bear*), and watches *Ôriôn*. Did he see nought but these ? Above him blazed the *Lion ;* in front were the *Twins* with *Prokyôn* on their left and the *Goat* (*Aix*) on their right. He noticed *Ôriôn* on the horizon at his right front; and, as he viewed the Pleiads, he would of necessity behold all these far more conspicuous stars, as well as the Hyads, which, as the poet mentions them elsewhere, it will probably be admitted that he saw. But, possibly some one will suggest that these other constellations were not named yet ? ' No more of that.' *Aix-Capella* was known as (Sum.) *Askar* (' the Goat') in the Euphrates Valley at least a couple of thousand years earlier ; and *Lion and Twins* were then grey with age. But I will not pursue the subject further here.

In Homer the *Dog* (of *Ôriôn*), whether also a con-

stellation or not, is certainly a single star, *Seirios*, in
whose name Aryan and Semitic derivations coalesce.
On the Aryan side he is 'the *Scorcher*' (as connected
with σείρός, etc.); on the Semitic, he is 'the Burning-
one,' 'Lamp,' etc. (as connected with the Ar. *sirâj*,
etc.), *Sirius* and *Procyon* being, as Prof. Hommel
has shown, 'the two Si'ray.' In *W.A.I.*, VI. vi. 19,
where the Ak. name is lost, we have the As.
equivalent *Kalbu Samas* ('Dog-of-the-Sun'); and in
W.A.I., II. xlix. 63, we find the *Kakkab Lik.-Udu*.
The As. *kakkabu*, Heb. *kôkhâbh* is used both for
'star' and 'constellation'; and therefore we have to
decide in every case by the context. We may read
either 'Star' or 'Constellation of the Dog of the
Sun' (Ak. *Lik-Udu*.). As a stellar *Dog* often appears
with other constellation-figures on the Euphratean
Boundary-stones (Vide *sup.* p. 173), I strongly incline
to the opinion that the Homeric *Kuôn* is also a constellation; just as in the case of the *Eagle*, alike in
Akkadian and in Greek, which repeats the Akkadian
terminology, we have the same name (*Eagle*) applied
both to the constellation and to its principal star
(Vide *inf.* p. 199).

It is noticeable that nearly the whole of the
personages and objects which make up the constellation-figures, are to be found in Homer. He
does not mention *Kêpheus*, but, according to
Athenaios (xiv. 32), he knew the name *Kassiepeia*,
and wrote (*Il.* viii. 305):—

Καλὴ Κασσιέπεια θεοῖς δέμας ἐοικυῖα.

And he introduces Eurynomê (*Ib.* xviii. 399), who is
merely a phase of Kassiepeia herself. Perseus is
'most famous of all men' (*Ib.* xiv. 320), whilst

the Gorgon head appears alike on the *aigis* of Athênê
and on the shield of Agamemnôn. It is certain,
therefore, that the poet knew the story of *Andromeda;* and he speaks of 'the Sea-monster' (*Kêtos,
Ib.* xx. 147) against which Hêraklês, a variant
phase of Perseus, fought, and says that Amphitrîtê
had 'many such' (*Od.* v. 421-2). Cheirôn (the
Centaur), Asklêpios (the *Snake-holder*), Ganymêdês
(often considered to be the *Water-* or *Wine-pourer*);
Atlas (= Ph. Atel, 'the Darkness,' sire of stars),
the heaven-supporter ; *Ôrîôn, Hêraklês* with *Bow*
and *Arrow;* the ship *Argô,* the beautiful Sidonian
Mixing-bowl (*Krêtêr, Il.* xxiii. 741); the *Dolphin,*
as a kind of king of fish (*Ib.* xxi. 22); the *Water-
snake* (*Ib.* ii. 723), the *Lion* and *Bull* (*Ib.* xvii. 542);
the *Eagle* and *Hare* (*Ib.* 674-8); the *Eagle* and *Swan*
(*Ib.* xv. 690-2) ; the *Bear,* the *Dog,* the *Twins*
(Kastôr and Polydeukês), are all familiar Homeric
figures. As of course, the poems speak of serpents,
horses, charioteers, archers, wreaths, lyres, birds,
rams, goats, virgins, doves, fishes, streams, altars and
tripods. They do not, I think, mention crabs (which,
however, appear in the *Batrachomyomachia*), crows,
or scorpions.

Margidda ('the Wain.' Vide *sup.* p. 169) was, in
the Euphratean scheme, specially connected with the
god Mul-lil (Vide *sup.* p. 154); and, in this aspect,
was called (Ak.) *Wul-mo-sarra* ('The Lord-the-
Voice-of-the-Firmament'), and, as a nocturnal manifestation of Mul-lil, (As.) *Bilu zakki mâti* ('The Lord-
of-the-Ghost-world.' *W.A.I.* II. xlviii. 56). This
description is especially interesting, as it enables us
to see how thoroughly Euphratean in origin are
many of the Iranian stellar fancies and beliefs.

In the Iranian scheme, *Haptôiriṅga*, 'the Seven-enthroned-ones' (= the *Wain*), the leader of the northern stars, is 'entrusted with the gate and passage of hell, to keep back those of the myriad demons, and demonesses, and fairies (Pairikas) and sorcerers (Yâtus) who are in opposition to the celestial sphere and constellations' (*Minokhired*, xlix. 15, ap. West). This is merely an expansion and intensification of *Margidda*, ruler of the ghosts. *Margidda* is translated by the Kretan Ἄγαννα· ἄμαξα ... καὶ ἡ ἐν οὐρανῷ Ἄρκτος (Hêsychios).

Judging by analogy, the Ak. name of the *Lesser Bear* would be **Marturra* ('the Little-chariot'), Bab.-As. *Rukubu* ('the Chariot'), Heb. *Rekhev*. Its seven stars are a smaller copy of those of the *Greater Bear*, and the star at the end of the tail (*a Ursae Min.*) is called *Alrucaba* ('the Chariot') in the *Alphonsine Tables*. Tem. B.C. 1300, *β Ursae Min.*, called ἡ Φοινίκη ('the Phoenician'-star), and now (Ar.) *Kaukab* ('*The* Star'), had succeeded *a Draconis* as Pole-star. Thalês, a man 'of the family of the Thelidai, who are Phoenicians by descent, among the most noble of all the descendants of Kadmos, as Platôn testifies' (Diog. Laert. *Thalês*, i), did not indeed 'discover' the *Lesser Bear*, but induced the Greeks to sail by it (Vide Schol. *Il.* xviii. 487 ; Aratos, *Phainom.* 37-44; Kallimachos, *Frag.* xciv). There is not the least reason to suppose that Homer was not acquainted with the *Lesser Bear;* but we may feel sure he would never have spoken of it with the grandiloquent inappropriateness of Euripidês, ' Twin *Bears* with the swift wandering rushes of their tails, guard the Atlanteian pole' (*Peirithoös*, Frag .iii). On the contrary the motion of the *Bears* is slow and

solemn, so that they have been called the *Biers*, and
they are by no means ' twins.' Yet the quotation
well illustrates the nurturing character of the *Ursa
Matronalis*; and, with a passage to the like effect
from Mr. Ruskin, I will conclude. Describing the
sculptures of ' the Tower of Giotto ' at Florence, he
says :—

' The next sculpture is of Eve spinning and Adam
hewing the ground into clods. . . Above them are
an oak and an apple-tree. Into the apple-tree a
little bear is trying to climb. . . The figure of the
bear is again represented by Jacopo della Quercia, on
the north door of the Cathedral of Florence. I am
not sure of its complete meaning ' (*Mornings in
Florence*, 4th edit. 1894, pp. 159-60).

The Bear trying to get the fatal apple is thus
connected with Eve, Universal Mother, the great
Ursa Matronalis. The animal appears on the coins
of Hadrianothera and Mantineia.

XXIX. The Constellation-figures as Coin-types

The last remark naturally leads us to notice that
alike on the coinage of Phoenicia, Lydia, Lykia,
Etruria and Hellas the constellation-figures appear
as coin-types; and that not here or there merely,
but all over the shores of the Mediterranean. Nor
is it a few of them that are found in this connexion ;
for there is not one which is entirely absent. After
making every allowance for special local circumstances, play on words, etc., the fact shows how well
known and respected the various Signs were from a

very early period. As I intend to treat of this
subject at length elsewhere, I shall here only take a
single city, Kyzikos in Mysia, as a specimen ; and
I think the reader will probably be surprised at the
result. Kyzikos, connected by colonization with
Milêtos, which latter place is said to have been
founded by Kretans, stood upon the ' Island of the
Bears ' (Ἄρκτων νῆσος), a name not without a constellational connexion (Vide *sup.* p. 64) ; and
possessed a coinage commencing in the seventh
century B.C. Amongst its coin-types are :—

Bowl. Bakchic *kantharos,* = *Krêtêr.*
Bucranium. Filleted. The Phoenician *Aleph* (Vide
sup. p. 182).
Bull. Stepping to r., walking, butting, kneeling,
winged.   This coin gave rise to the proverbial saying
on purchased silence, βοῦς ἐπὶ γλώσσε βέβηκεν (Cf.
Aischylos, *Ag.* 36).
Charioteer. Erichthonios, presented to Athêna.
Crab. Holding head of *Fish* in claws.
Dog. *Statant,* r. fore-paw raised.
Dog. Twy-headed, *statant,* with tail ending in head
of *Serpent.* A very curious and interesting figure.
The Twy-headed-dog with serpentine body appears
on the Euphratean Boundary-stones (Vide R. B. Jr.,
The Heavenly Display, Fig. lxiv.), and was a symbol
of Tu or Tutu, the Death-god.   Mr. W. Wroth
wrongly calls this *Dog* Kerberos.
Dolphin. Bearing youthful male figure (Melikertês-
Palaimôn. Cf. Paus. II. i. 7).
—— On r. hand of Poseidôn.
Eagle. Head of, with *Tunny* in beak.
Fish. The protagonistic type of the place is the

Tunny; and we find from Schol. Arat. *Phainom.*
242, that the *Northern* of the two zodiacal *Fish*
Χαλδαῖοι καλοῦσιν Ἰχθὺν χελιδονίαν. The *Chelidonias*
was a kind of tunny. I do not suggest (and this
principle holds good in many similar instances that
the people of Kyzikos stamped their coins with a
tunny merely because they knew it as a zodiacal
Sign. But their fishing industry harmonized in the
matter with their constellational knowledge ; and
both jointly contributed to this particular selection of
type, of which the coins show many variants, *e.g.* :—

Naked male figure with body ending in fish's tail,
= Êa-Dagôn-Poseidôn (Vide *sup.* p. 128) ; beneath,
Tunny. Êa ('Water-house') = the Ἀὸς of Damaskios,
the Ὤης of Helladios, the Ὠάννης of Bêrôsos, explained by Lenormant as *Êa-χan* ('Êa-the-Fish'),
and by Lacouperie as if from a reading *A-e-anu,*
viz., Anu-Êa ('the god Êa') read reversely (Cf.
Khasis-adra and *Adra-khasis,* etc.). I may remark
that certain Greek transliterations represent Semitic
names read backwards way on. This, of course,
arises from the fact that Semitic is read from r. to l.,
Greek from l. to r. The Ak. god-name *Da-gan*
means 'the Exalted-one' (Ak. *da,* 'summit,' + *gan,*
'the participle of the substantive verb.' Sayce.).
Various Semitic etymologies were subsequently
attached to the word, *e.g., dâgân,* 'corn' (Sanchou.
i. 5) and *dag,* 'fish.' The cult of the primeval
Fish-god of Lower Babylonia passed westward to the
Phoenician seaboard ; and thence to Hellas, island
and continental. The *Tunny* is specially connected
in art with Poseidôn (Vide Athen. viii. 36). And in
illustration of the fact that the zodiacal *Pisces* were
tunnies, we find, in the Ducal Palace at Venice,

Jupiter 'represented in his houses Sagittarius and Pisces . . . raises his sceptre in his left hand over Sagittarius, represented as the centaur Chiron, [= Êabani, *sup.* p. 178]; and holds two tunnies in his right' (Ruskin, *Stones of Venice*, ii. 353).

Winged female figure, holding *Tunny* in r. hand. As figures of the archaic Poseidôn are often incorrectly described as ' Tritôn,' ' Glaukos,' etc., so figures such as this, in default of anything else, are frequently called 'Nikê.' It is more probably a type derived from the Phoenician Adâmâth—*Andromeda*, which celestially is next to the *Tunny*.

Goat. Head of.
Hêraklês. Bearded (= the Gilgames-type), naked, kneeling on one knee (= Engonasin), with *Club*, *Bow*, and two *Arrows*.
—— Wearing *Lion*-skin, strangling *Lion*, etc.
Horse. ' Pegasus ' (= Sem. *Pegah*, ' bridle.' Bérard. *I.e.*, the Horse caught and bridled), with pointed wing, flying r. *Pêgasos* appears on a Hittite seal.
Lion. With Hêraklês; scalp of, *affronté*, etc.
Ram. *Statant*, kneeling.
Scorpion. In small incuse square.
Tripod. Cf. *Deltôton* (*Sup.* p. 171).

We also find Apollôn with *Lyre*, Dionysos, and Harmodios and Aristogeitôn, who are certainly excellent representatives of the *Twins*. A Satyr, pouring wine from a jar into a *kanthar*, cannot be considered as a symbol of *Aquarius;* but, with this exception, every Sign of the Zodiac, as well as many other constellation-figures are practically represented on the coins of this single city.

13

We find together, alike on coins and in the sky, *Hêraklês* and the *Arrow ; Hêraklês* and the *Serpent ; Eagle* and *Dolphin ; Pêgasos* and *Fish ; Snake-holder* and *Snake ;* two *Fishes ; Lion* (-skin), *Water-snake,* and *Crab,* etc. This immense use of the constellation-figures is the result neither of accident nor of caprice. It points to a recognition of astronomy as nothing less than a phase of religion.

XXX. Harekhal and the Stymphalian Birds

Ere leaving the subject of Greek constellation-myths, let us notice one of them in some detail. The Aryanistic mythologist, when speaking of the labours of Hêraklês, observes :—

'The Stymphalides or birds of the lake near Stymphâlos in Arkadia are called the offspring of Ares. Their destruction by Hêraklês seems to have had a purely local origin' (*C.* p. 620).

In other words, he is quite unable even to suggest any explanation of the legend. The totemistic mythologist— But we must not expect explanations from him. Mr. Farnell innocently remarks, 'Arcadia lies remote from Oriental influences ' (*Cults,* ii. 430). On the contrary, as M. Bérard has shown, in very great detail, it was at one time almost a mass of Phoenician ideas and cult; and it is the scene of many of the doings of Harekhal ('*The* Traveller,' vide *sup.* p. 99), so often assisted by his faithful hench-man Iolâos (= Ph. Iol, 'contractum ex Iubal, Iual, splendor Baalis.' Gesenius. Cf. the Phoenician settlement at Iol-kos in S. Thessaly, near 'the Athamantic field,' vide *sup.* p. 146), and attended by

various Arkadians. In illustration of the hero's
name, we find, in the *Etymol. Mag.* in voc. Γάδειρα
(= Ph. *Gadir*, 'an enclosure,' Gk. τα Γάδειρα, Lat.
Gadês, Span. Cadiz.), a place near the Pillars of
Heraklês and said to have been founded by him, and
which contained famous temples of Heraklês and
Kronos, . . . ὡς φησὶ Κλαύδιος Ἰούλιος ἐν ταῖς Φοινίκης
ἱστορίαις, ὅτι Ἀρχαλεὺς υἱὸς Φοίνικος κτίσας πόλιν,
ὠνόμασε τῇ Φοινίκων γραφῇ. This writer, of unknown
date, the author of the *Phoinikika*, was named, not
' Julius,' but ' Iolâos.'

The Stymphalian Bird-legend is as follows :—A
flock of demon-, human-flesh-eating, man-slaying
Birds, daughters of Stymphâlos and Ornis, and
nourished by Arês, had fled from some Wolves to the
Stymphalian Lake. Eurystheus having ordered
Heraklês to expel them, he either slew them with his
arrows, or drove them away. They were subse-
quently found by the Argonauts in the island of
Aretias (' the Unblest '). Such, briefly, is the dream.
What is the interpretation ?

The progress of the Phoenicians northwards from
their station at Kythêra (Vide *sup.* p. 131) has been
very ably illustrated by M. Bérard, and can be
followed in Pausanias by him who reads that author
with understanding. On the Lakonian coast lay
Sidê (= Tsidôn, Σιδὼν) and Hêlos, founded by
Hêlios, son of Perseus, *i.e.*, the Phoenician Sun-god.
In the Eurôtas Valley was the ancient town of Amy-
klai (*Il.* ii. 584), whose mythic founder Amyklas =
the Kypriot and Ph. Resheph (' the Thunder-bolt ')—
Mikal, the celestial fire ; and whose son, the beautiful
Hyakinthos (= Adônis), slain in his youth, was there
honoured at the great festival of the Hyakinthia.

13 *

Passing northwards we reach the Phoenician fortress of Lykosoura, 'oldest of towns' (Paus. VIII. xxxviii. 1), and the dread sanctuary of Zeus Lykaios with his human-sacrifice cult (*Ib.* VIII. ii. 1 ; xxxviii. 5) ; near which is Phigaleia (= Sem. Phegâ, 'fortune,' + Êl, 'the Fortune of Êl.' Cf. Pagiel), a famous centre of non-Aryan divinities (Vide *sup.* p. 41) and of magical and necromantic rites (*Ib.* III. xvii. 8), and said to have been founded by a child of Lykâôn (Hêsych. *in voc.*). Crossing the Alphaios ('the Bull' river), and noting such names as Makaria (= the town of Melqârth), and Orchomenos, which also occurs as a place-name in Boiôtia, we arrive at Stymphâlos. The exploits of Hêraklês were commemorated in this Arkadian region. On the wall of the temple of the Semitic goddess, whose name was rendered by Despoina ('the Mistress'), at Akakesion, was represented that great exploit of the Semitic hero, the robbing the Aryan Apollôn of his Tripod (Vide *sup.* p. 97). And the contest between the two divinities is further illustrated by the legend that the Lakonian Aristodêmos was shot with arrows by Apollôn, because he had consulted Hêraklês, instead of going to the oracle of the god (Paus. III. i. 5). As the Phoenician influence passed over into Êlis, we hear of a dread contest between Hêraklês and the Aryan Aïdôneus at Pylos (*Il.* v. 398-402 ; Paus. VI. xxv. 3), *i.e.*, primarily the 'Gate' of the Under-world, forced by the conquering Sun-god. In Lakônikê Harekhal-Archaleus also appears as Argalos, eldest son of Amyklas (Paus. III. i. 3).

'Stymphâlos, the founder of the town, was the third in descent from Arkas the son of Kallistô'

(*Ib.* VÍII. xxii. 1) ; and the three generations of the mythic pedigree afford some indication of the time which it took the Phoenicians to penetrate to this locality. The name is very interesting. Thus, we find ' *Stembal,* filius Masinissae Polyb. 37, 3, ubi editum est Στέμβανον (lege Στέμβαλον). Contractum est ex *Mastanabal* ' (Gesen. *Script. Ling. Ph.* p. 414), ' prob. clypeus Baalis' (*Ib.* 410),= the peculiar Boiôtian Buckler of Hêraklês, Lat. *clypeus,* always found on the Boiôtian coinage. *Stembâlos* = *Stymphâlos.* Near this very ancient town (Cf. *Il.* ii. 608), then, clearly of Phoenician foundation, is located the scene of the contest between Hêraklês and the Demon-birds. On a Florentine Gem, generally figured in illustrations of the twelve labours of Hêraklês, he is shown, kneeling on one knee (the attitude of Gilgames-*Engonasin*), about to discharge an arrow at the three Birds, who are advancing in a line against him. Says Pausanias :—' Concerning the Stymphâlos river there is a tradition that once man-eating birds lived there; and these birds Hêraklês is said to have killed with his arrows. But Peisandros of Kameiros (Vide *sup.* p. 170) says that Hêraklês did not kill the birds, but only scared them away with rattles ' (VIII. xxii. 4). He adds that there were similar birds in Arabia; and that the birds were represented on the roof of the ancient temple of Stymphalian Artemis. The coin-types of the place are Hêraklês in Lion-skin ; Same, striking with Club, holding Lion-skin and Bow; Same, with strung bow and quiver ; Head and neck of crested Bird ; and Head of Artemis. We observe that Peisandros, an early Eastern Hellene, was familiar with the story, and knew a special variant of it.

Now this great exploit of Harekhal-Hêraklês is

grandly commemorated in the Phoenician celestial
sphere, which is also our own. There *Hêraklês-
Engonasin*, kneeling, shoots an *Arrow* (= the constellation *Oïstos-Sagitta*) against the three Bird-constel-
lations, the *Eagle*, the *Vulture* (also called the *Lyre*),
and the *Bird* (*Ornis*), otherwise called the *Swan*
(*Kyknos*, another personage killed in battle by
Hêraklês). Now we see how it was that the concept
of the constellation the *Arrow* arose (Vide *sup*. p. 163),
and why it was not imagined as a sceptre or a lance,
and why its point is turned from Hêraklês and
towards the Birds. Now we see, when Otfried Müller
said there was 'nothing mythological' about the
Arrow, and that it was so named from its 'figure,'
how profoundly ignorant he was respecting the origin
of this, as of many other, constellations. How silly
now appears the idle notion that someone looked at
these particular stars, and thought, independently of
any further or other idea, that they resembled an
arrow. Their real resemblance to an arrow was thus
utilized in recording the contest of Hêraklês and the
Birds. 'Steel-blue Vega, the zenith-queen of the
heavenly Lyre,' as I say elsewhere, is called *Al-Nesr-
al-Wâki* (Vide Ulugh Beigh's *Star Catalogue* in voc.),
Vultur cadens, 'the Falling Grype,' and the *Wega*
of the *Alphonsine Tables*. According to an Arab
commentator on Ulugh Beigh, the stars є and ζ *Lyrae*
represent the two wings of the 'Grype,' by drawing
in which he lets himself swiftly down to the earth.
And this Phoenician myth of Harekhal and the Birds
is but a reduplication of the original Euphratean
myth, according to which Marduk-Merôdach, with
whom Gilgames, as a solar hero, is identical, fights
with and overcomes three Demon-birds, as shown on

the Cylinders (Vide Lajard, *Culte de Mithra*, Pl. lxi. Fig. 7), or contends with his arrows against a single Bird (*Ibid.* Pl. liv. B. 11). Sometimes a god is portrayed standing between two Ostriches, holding each by the neck (Cullimore, *Oriental Cylinders* No. XL), *i.e.*, restraining the unruly powers of nature. For the Birds of Stymphâlos are the raging Storm-birds (Vide *sup.* p. 176), hostile to, and overcome by, the warrior Sun-god Merôdach-Gilgames-Harekhal. I may add that the star we call the *Eagle*, *i.e.*, *Altair* (= Ar. *Al-Tair*, 'the Bird,' *a Aquilae*), is so named because it was the *Idkhu* or *Erigu*, (' Powerful-bird,' *i.e.*, *Eagle*) of the Euphratean sphere ; whilst the *Vulture* was the Euphratean star *Raditartakhu* ('The-Snatching-swooping-tearing-bird') or Lämmergeier. Tartakhu, Heb. Tartak, LXX. Θαρθὰκ, was worshipped by the men of Ivah (Avites, 2 *Kings*, xvii. 31).

These Stymphalian Birds of storm and darkness had fled from Wolves ; and here we meet with the familiar play on words λευκός-λύκος, just as Apollôn, the *Light*-king, is besought to be as fierce as a *wolf*. Of course the Birds fly from the Light-rays, just as, conversely, the solar Athamas receives hospitality from Wolves. As of course, also, the Birds are killed, and are merely frightened away. Both statements are equally true ; storm and darkness perish, and again return. Play on words has ever pleased the mind, witness that ancient joke *Bab-ili* ('Gate-of-the-gods')-*Babel* ('Confusion,' *Gen.* xi. 9), which some people still take seriously ; and it also admirably lends itself to symbolism, and ultimately, in many cases, to confusion of thought. Thus, Lykaôn (= the votary of the Phoenician Baal), having sacri-

ficed an infant to Zeus Lykaios (= Laphystios, 'the
Glutton'—for human sacrifices), became, 'they say,
a wolf instead of a man' (Paus. VIII. ii. 1), an
illustration of Hellenic horror at Phoenician ritual.
Here the 'untutored anthropologist' will of course
see cannibalism, lycanthropy, and heaven knows what.
Thus, again, according to Plutarch (*Peri Is.* lxxii),
in Egypt the Lykopolites alone ate sheep, 'because
the Wolf, which they revere as a deity, does so.'
Let us take this statement for what it may be worth;
but why did the Lycopolites revere the Wolf? As
a totem-ancestor? No, as a symbol of the Sun-god
(Vide Macrob. *Sat.* I. xvii. 40-1, for a reference to
the cult, and the play on words). Call this kind
of thing 'a disease of language,' or what you will.
There it is, a familiar factor in the situation.

Such, then, gentle reader, is the legend of Harekhal
and the Stymphalian Birds. You perceive which
system can explain it, and which systems cannot.
If the Aryan Zeus be right, follow him ; but, if Baal
for once be the proper god, then follow him.

XXXI. Roman divinity-names

The same difficulty which we encounter in Hellas
in determining whether this or that god-name and
god be Aryan or non-Aryan, we find also at Rome.
Just as the religion of Hellas is a combination of
Aryan and non-Aryan (Semitic) influences, so is the
religion of Rome a combination of Aryan and non-
Aryan (Etruscan) influences, + Hellenic importations.
We know that Ju-piter = Ζεὺς-πατήρ both historically
and philologically, that in origin both were the same

personage.   We are equally well aware that the Lat.
Jupiter = Et. Tina, Tinia, as analogue, *i.e.*, each
being the principal god in his respective Pantheon.
I have further endeavoured to show that the Et.
Tinia represents an original form *Tingiara*, which =
the Sum. *Dingira* (= 'creator,' then 'god'); and
that both are variant phases of the archaic Turanian
word meaning 'sky,' 'god,' 'creator,' which we find
in such forms as the Ak. *dimer*, Sum. *gingiri*
('goddess'), *Gingira* ('the goddess Istar'), Yakute
tangara, Mongol *tengri*, Hunnish *tangli*, Turkish
tangry, Tchagatai *tingri*, Chinese *tien* (all meaning
'sky,' 'sky-god,' 'god'), Finnic *tie* (-Jumala),
Magyar (Is)-*ten* ('god'), etc.   And we may now also
take it for granted that the desperate efforts of the
last 200 years to prove that Etruscan is an Aryan
language are abandoned, except possibly by one or
two savants whose lives have been wasted over them.
But when we examine the names, concepts, and
history of various members of the Roman Pantheon,
it is exceedingly difficult to determine their origin
with any certainty.   Take the case of Minerva = Et.
Menrva.   The history of the goddess tells us nothing
which decides the point.   She is not found amongst
the other branches of the Aryan Family; and we are
therefore left with the name alone.   The difficulties
connected with it will be appreciated when the
student has studied Prof. Müller, *Lects. Sci. Lang.*
ii. 552, combined with Canon Is. Taylor, *Etruscan
Researches*, p. 135 *et seq.*   I merely instance this
Roman question as an illustration of the fact, that
the presence of non-Aryan divinities in the Pantheon
of an Aryan nation, is by no means an abnormal
phenomena.

XXXII. Conclusion

And here I bring this illustrative sketch of the principles of the Aryo-Semitic School of Hellenic Mythologists to a close.   The instances given are not exhaustive, but simply by way of example ; and the treatment is very brief.   But enough has been said to show an unprejudiced reader that our system is not dependent upon this or that etymology, is not a chain whose strength is but that of some dubious and fragile link.   It is held together by the three-fold cord of history, mythology and philology, supported in a most valuable manner by art and archaeology ; which latter studies can give no assistance to the maker of Greek and Vedic comparisons.   It is not a bygone system, resting upon an exploded philology, or upon complete ignorance of modern discoveries. It is thoroughly up to date ; and every newly trans-lated cuneiform tablet, every fresh Phoenician inscription, every Hittite find, every further relic of antiquity laid bare by the spade, Mykenaean civiliza-tion, Kretan pictograph, Egyptian papyrus, will but confirm and strengthen it.   I have not thought it necessary in these pages to speak in detail of the various gifts, beginning with letters, conferred by the Semitic East upon Hellas.   They are known to every student ; and I venture to think that if Prof. Müller should ever read this work, he will see that our theory and standpoint are not based merely on a few bold comparisons, such as Peleg and Pelasgos ; but that we have some reason alike for the faith, and for the want of faith, that is in us.

As to Mr. Lang, who 'gives no quarter to his adversaries' (Vide *sup.* p. 78), we have nothing to fear from him.   Mr. Casaubon himself is as likely to refute us. A man of his abilities and great position in journalism can for a time, assisted of course by disciples, produce what he himself has styled a 'backwater.' But no empty sack of a system can stand upright by itself ; and the totemism of the 'untutored anthropologist' is necessarily destined to an absolute collapse. If people believe in it for the moment, ·we are not discouraged. Truth, as Prof. Müller says, is in no hurry. She is not dead, although at times she may be sleeping. We

> 'Remember how the course of Time will swerve,
> Crook and turn upon itself in many a backward streaming
> curve.'

Doubtless Mr. Lang, as the critic, anonymous or otherwise, 'gives no quarter' to the author who is bound and gagged before him. As poor Mr. Joseph Jacobs, who had audaciously ventured to poach upon Mr. Lang's preserve of fairy tales, remarked, in the *Academy :*—

'I know nothing more damaging, and at the same time irritating, than to be reviewed by Mr. Andrew Lang,' because, although his corrections are excellent, 'the impression they leave is, as I think, so abominably unjust by their want of proportion between the few words of general and external praise, and the huge remainder of specific fault-finding.'

Yet Mr. Jacobs was so terrified at Mr. Lang's very awful threat never to review his volumes again, that he apologises, and defines his Reviewer as 'the foremost figure among contemporary English [There is some pleasantry here.] men of letters.' Notwithstanding that he is such a 'fearful wildfowl' as all this, I don't feel much terror of Mr. Lang. For, routed by his Mouse, deserted by his Bear, and snarled at by his Wolf, whose ears it is neither safe to hold nor to let go, he seems in somewhat evil plight at present ; and I fear, from divers indications, will fall a victim to the Corn-spirit. I see only one chance for him. Let him abandon mythology again (Vide *sup.* p. 78), say, for the next twenty years (he may, of course, read it up a little quietly), and take another severe course of the Cock Lane Ghost and Co., or join a special midnight tour with that valiant lady who, according to his entertaining pages, makes appointments with spectres at 1 a.m. in churches in Lincolnshire. Should he ever include in such travels either of the fine old shrines that adorn this town, I shall be happy,—not to give him a bed, he won't want that,—but breakfast after he has made a night of it. Meanwhile, I say, as touching mythology, Let the light enter.

APPENDIX A

PROFESSOR AGUCHEKIKOS
ON TOTEMISM

(Reprinted from the edition of 1886)

From the BUNKUMVILLE ANTHROPOLOGICAL GAZETTE, April 1st,
A.D. 4886

> ‘ Now attest
> That those, whom you call’d fathers, did beget you.’
> —*Shakspere*

IT is with sincere pleasure that we hail the appearance
of the twentieth and concluding Volume of Professor
Aguchekikos’ brilliant work, *Anglican Totemism in the
Victorian Epoch*, which has just been translated into
American by our learned fellow-countryman, Dr. Driveller.
If the contemplation of European man at a somewhat remote
period is rather calculated to depress the mind ; if these
interesting researches into the history of idiotic, but at the
same time remarkably inventive, distant connexions might
be deemed by the profane to throw some shadow, however
slight, upon Columbia herself, such a feeling will more than
disappear when, with just self-complacency, we contrast
our own intelligence with the Anglican imbecility of the
Victorian Epoch. At that period even the great Republic
was not quite the country she is now, when the entire

continent is divided between ourselves in the north and the Mikado of Tierra del Fuego in the south. But, even then, we were immeasurably in front of Britain, a land where, as Professor Aguchekikos, a savant of whom New Athens may well be proud, shows on almost every page, totemism reigned supreme.

Totemism, as the Professor reminds us, is the belief that one is descended from any natural object except man and woman ; and this opinion, the intrinsic probability of which will immediately carry its acceptance to an enlightened mind, was once universal, as is shown by many a senseless old story and bit of meaningless legend, but, above all, by the animal-names that have come down to us. Man in early times was an Evolutionist of the severest type.

Now, although the study of language, and the deductions that used to be drawn from it in the pre-scientific period are, on the whole, rather more worthless than the art of table-turning, yet in one respect, and in one only, linguistic research has been truly valuable ; it has revealed the names upon which ancient totemism is based. True it is that all other ancient name-study is ridiculous, for the obvious and unanswerable reason that everybody is not agreed about the meaning of every name. But the totemist is justified in making an exception in favour of totem-names, or otherwise, as Professor Aguchekikos well observes, ancient totemism itself would disappear altogether. We are thus enabled to feel a rational confidence that, if thousands of years ago a man was called by some name bearing more or less resemblance to words now used to signify ' mouse,' his name actually was Mouse ; and further, that he regarded a veritable mouse as having been his great-grandfather.

These considerations also indirectly involve another law which, we are happy to say, is now ' no longer a theory, but a generally recognized fact,' namely—*The belief of man in early times ran exactly contrary to his experience.* Thus, as he had never seen or known a bear or a mouse bring forth boys and girls, he necessarily concluded that these animals had done so in the past, and justly argued that what has once happened may happen again. True it is, as the Professor notes, that in the pre-scientific period before the wisdom of the 'untutored anthropologist' was universally allowed, people thought that the beliefs of early man were the result of his observation and experience, but no one is so dull as to entertain such a notion nowadays. The next point about each tribal totem or revered ancestral object is that it might not be eaten by any of the tribe. A very ancient but delightful writer, and one, moreover, centuries in advance of his time, has given us a singularly striking instance of the appropriateness of this regulation, in reminding us that 'among well-known totems none is more familiar than the sun.' Had not the above rule been strictly observed in early days, even such men as Professor Aguchekikos and Dr. Driveller must have been at present completely in the dark.

The totemist had a further prohibition, namely, that members of the same stock or tribe having the same totem, as a rule, might not intermarry. Thus, in a tribe having a Crane as their totem, a man whose name was Crane might not marry a Miss Crane; and it is highly interesting to find from many thousand examples cited by the Professor (Vide Vol. xviii., pp. 1-1200), that this regulation was strictly adhered to in Britain throughout the Victorian Epoch. The Professor tells us that, after prolonged research, he cannot meet with a single authentic instance of a Mr. Bull marrying a Miss Bull, or a Mr. Crane marrying a Miss Crane; whilst, on the other hand, he had met with a case of a Mr. Crane marrying a Miss Lamb, a girl of course belonging to another totem tribe.

But a totem, as the Professor shows, need not even be an animal; and we have strong reasons for believing that at the remote epoch in question a Thistle was the great totem of the northern part of the island of Britain, just as Plutarch tells us (or more shame for him if he doesn't), that some Athenians believed they were descended from an Asparagus-plant, a vegetable which Dr. Driveller informs us in a foot-note, is supposed to be identical with the *Frutex Curiosus* or 'Rum Shrub.'

Such, then, is totemism; and as there are animals, plants, and other natural objects all over the world, we see that it necessarily prevailed in every country in early times. Man was not then ' prosing about the weather,' or examining the face of nature. Like the soldiers in Giglio's army (to quote from a historical romance called *The Rose and the Ring*, attributed to the semi-mythical writer Thackeray), he scarcely noticed the difference between day-light and dark; and paid no great attention to the sun beyond declining to eat it. The stars, however, did come in for some share of his observation; and, as anyone who will look at them sees at once that their groups don't in the least resemble bears, lions, or any other animals; so, as the Professor well shows, acting on the same great law, in accordance with which, as noticed, early belief was exactly contrary to experience, man at once necessarily concluded that the stars were literally bears, lions, etc., and accordingly spoke of the *Bear*, the *Lion*, and other sky animals, even in the Victorian Epoch. Are we entitled to say that the Britishers did not really suppose there was an actual lion in the sky at night? Not in the least. As the Professor points out, the present belief (whatever it may really be) of the Kakoriboos is decisive on the question.

So deep is the obscurity of antiquity that, even after the efforts of almost a lifetime, the Professor seems doubtful whether a Lion or a Bull was the national totem of South Britain in the Victorian Epoch; and he has in vain tried to decide the question by a searching investigation whether their flesh was eaten, and which was least popular at dinner parties. Dr. Driveller remarks in a foot-note, that no one ate Bull who could get anything else.

In the part of the island then called Wales there is a similar doubt between the Goat and the Onion; and here the Professor well reminds us that Pliny states the Egyptians swore by the Onion whilst others are said to have sworn at it. It is almost certain that, at the period in question onions were eaten in some places; and even in a then former age, Herodotus (ever a trustworthy authority) speaks of the vast number of onions devoured by the Great Pyramid Builders. But in Britain the Onion was doubtless eaten only in contempt and defiance of the Welsh, or other tribes who had an onion totem. Shakspere, a verse writer and tale-inventor, who lived somewhere about the time, describes one Pistol, an enemy to the Welsh, as eating a leek. This same writer, who seems to have had a fair amount of talent for an early European, nevertheless affords a melancholy illustration of the folly of the human mind of the period. As the Professor shows by many quotations from his works (which have been preserved in America), he believed that Day was a gaudily-dressed, chattering child, with a somewhat tender conscience; and that the Sea was a woman in whose bosom the child slept at eventide (2 *Henry VI., iv.* 1); that the Stars were candles put in the sky by a person called Night (*Romeo and Juliet, iii.* 5); that the Sun was drawn in a coach (*Titus Andron. ii.* 1) by flame-footed horses (*Romeo and Juliet, iii.* 2), and so on. Such a state of mind seems very strange to us now, but we understand it at once when we remember the remarks of the traveller Von Poddingcoft, on what is supposed to be the present state of mind of the Kakoriboos.

The Professor justly, but yet perhaps almost unnecessarily, reprobates the foolish habit which formerly prevailed amongst the now happily extinct class of philologists and comparative mythologists of quoting from ancient documents, sacred books, inscriptions, and the like, it being as impossible to make either head or tail of any of them as it is to say what was the meaning of the word 'Zeus.' If any caviller should be hardy enough to enquire 'Why, then, does the Professor indulge in the above quotations?' let him remember that, as in philology (otherwise worthless), an exception is made as above noticed, in favour of totem-names, so, as regards ancient literature of all kinds, the scientifically untutored anthropologist of course accepts

14

anything which seems to bring grist to his mill, and rightly rejects the rest.

A few more details culled from the Professor's brilliant pages respecting the totemistic Britain of the Victorian Epoch cannot fail to be of interest. Thus, it is strange to learn that even in the City of London, which might have been fairly regarded as the very centre of knowledge, totemism prevailed almost universally. Two totem clans especially, the Bulls and the Bears, seem to have fiercely opposed each other in a struggle which, like the Hittite wars of old, lasted for centuries. The causes of this contest are very obscure; but we read that it was connected with a 'stock exchange.' This at once reminds us of tree totemism, and Dr. Driveller, in a valuable note, refers to the ancient practice of the Hebrews of asking 'counsel of their stocks.' The ingenious and highly probable conclusion at which the Professor arrives is that the two tribes decided for some (unknown) reason to exchange their stocks or totems, but that disputes arose in carrying out the arrangement. With reference to Bull-totems the most untutored anthropologist will at once remember the golden calf of Aaron, the wooden bull of Daedalus, the ox-headed Astarte, the bull-horned Bacchus, the cow-horned Isis and Io, and many others. The Bears, too, were an ancient clan; one Samuel Johnson is said to have been a prominent member of it.

Very many totem tribes existed in Britain at the Victorian Epoch. Amongst others the Professor mentions the clans of Bear, Bull, Bullock, Bird, Buzzard, Bee, Crane, Crow, Dove, Ducker, Duckham, Fish, Finch, Gooseman, Gosling, Hawk, Hogg, Jay, Lamb, Marten, Otter, Pike, Pigg, Salmon, Steer, Swallow, Wren, and Norfolk-Howard. The rigidity with which the principles of totemism were observed is well shown by the fact that no single instance can be adduced in which clans bearing the names of Buzzard, Bee, Crow, Finch, Hawk, Jay, Marten, Swallow, Wren, and Norfolk-Howard, ate the flesh of these creatures. The

Norfolk-Howard totem at once reminds the untutored anthropologist of Baal-zebub the totem of Ekron, which, as everybody knows, was only a big blue-bottle. Dr. Driveller, in a note, well conjectures that the Blue-bottle and Norfolk-Howard totems were carried about the country ; for the former seems also to have been known in Britain where there was a popular saying, ' The (blue) bottle stands with you,' *i.e.*, for the time being. He adds, too, that it is certain that Flies, which were not literal insects, were moved about in some of the towns. It is strange that we do not find the Mouse as a British totem ; but this is probably to be accounted for by the awe with which, as in Egypt, the Cat was held. In Britain even the most desperate criminals were greatly afraid of it.

Comparative mythologists used (oddly enough) to think that divinities were called Smintheus (' Mouse '-god), Parnopios (' Locust '-god), and the like, because they were supposed to defend mankind against the ravages of such creatures, as indeed ancient, but justly-forgotten, authors state (Vide Strabo, xiii. 64 ; Pausanias, i. 24). But we now see at once (or at all events ought to do so) that men thought they were descended, or had ascended, from mice and locusts ; and, if this seem very strange to us, we may remember that sailors in the Victorian Epoch would, still more strangely, speak of a comrade as being ' the son of a gun.'

Amongst other absurd notions which the Professor shows then prevailed in Britain was one which is said to have been not unknown among the Etruscans ; namely, that the souls of animals when sacrificed ascend to heaven as gods.

The Priest, it seems, was accustomed to say to a sacrificer who had not paid the full fee or ' duty,'—' Twopence more, and up goes the donkey.' Untutored Anthropologists will remember that this belief is treated of by Labeo, in his familiar work *De diis quibus origo animalis est.* The Professor himself has also dealt with it in a separate monograph on the ancient mysteries, entitled, *The Umbrella-stand in the Entrance Hall : a Study of the British Museum.*

14 *

That profound ignorance of the habits of animals which is so characteristic of the modern savage, also obtained almost universally in Britain at this unhappy Epoch. Thus, even in a grave and philosophical Journal called *Punch* (a word of unknown meaning), some fragments of which have survived, lion cubs were pictorially represented as bearing arms, and marching like soldiers under the leadership of an old lion. But, in this instance, as in nearly all others, we notice that belief ran exactly contrary to experience.

Someone somewhere says that Jupiter became an ant; and, similarly, the Professor has discovered that an ant-totem likewise existed in Britain. We hear of one Emmett, a Yorkshireman, who is said to have been also celebrated as a cricket, or cricketer as some termed it. Dr. Driveller observes, in a note, that there seems to have been some confusion between insects here; and, indeed, confusion is necessarily not altogether absent from totemistic research. We have mentioned Jupiter; and several funny stories were formerly current in Britain about him. The meaning of his name is of course unimportant, and besides, is necessarily unknown; but one writer of that age said (in the *Encyclopaedia Britannica*—ever the highest authority in matters mythological) that he was a king of the family of the Titans, and reigned in Krete. The general idea of him, however, was that he was a layman who was fond of reading the lessons in church; and 'The Lesson of Jupiter' was a familiar expression of the time. Untutored Anthropologists differ as to whether it was the first or the second or (possibly even the third) lesson which he read; and certainly it does not seem to have been much attended to in some quarters.

In one respect, and in one only, do the ancient totemists appear to have surpassed us moderns; and this, curiously enough, was in their power of invention. Even here, however, some of the writers in our evening newspapers and a certain section of Anthropologists run them hard. We find from the Professor's researches that the savage ancestors of the Chaldaeans, Greeks, Anglicans, and other ancient nations 'invented' the filthy and senseless stories which have since passed current as mythology and religion in order to supply 'amusing narrative.' It was certainly extremely kind of these poor people to take such trouble thus to entertain their contemporaries and posterity; but, at the same time, it must be admitted that they have incurred a somewhat serious responsibility by so doing, inasmuch as they have beguiled the time for their successors in more senses than one. Here, as in so many other instances, experience shows that to mean well is almost always equivalent to doing badly. It is a little odd, too, that these senseless and somewhat Rabelaisian tales were forthwith accepted by the Priesthood, and cherished as the most sacred mysteries of the faith. But so it was.

We rejoice to find, on such high authority, that the stories in question *are* meaningless, and that to examine them is *chercher raison où il n'y en a pas;* (1) because this view saves so much trouble; and (2) because all we see and know of man in later times confirms our belief in his habit of absolutely inventing things apropos of nothing. Thus, in the pre-scientific period laborious triflers professed to work out the alleged slow and strictly natural (as opposed to 'inventive') processes by which the art of writing, the alphabet, or the ideas about the ancient constellations had (as they declared) gradually arisen. Never again, fortunately, shall we work on lines such as these. Some nameless necessarily nameless (for we do not know that any particular name, not being a totem-name, is really ancient, and people talked about kings and queens long before there had been any), benefactor filled with this excellent wish to amuse, 'invented' the art of writing and jotted down an alphabet; and some other equally worthy soul (popularly supposed to have been a Chaldaean shepherd undisturbed by foot-and-mouth disease) looking up at the sky, which, somehow, he must necessarily have regarded as a man, reeled off the eight-and-forty old constellations—the *Ram, Bull, Twins,* and all the rest of them, in a style which, as Mr. Pickwick observed of the pleasantries of Mr. Peter Magnus, 'must have been calculated to afford his friends the highest gratification,' although at the same time it has greatly mystified posterity. For, what truly untutored anthropologists would trouble to investigate whether such things ever really had any meaning? Certainly not the enlightened 'dabblers who mark with a pencil the pages of travellers and missionaries.' If the question 'How did the stars get their names?' must be asked, as the Professor justly replies, 'Men gave them those names,' and because it was 'their nature to,' and there's an end of the matter.

It is a golden rule, and one strongly laid down by the Professor, to assume that anything which we cannot understand has no meaning. No other principle can really save self-respect; for, if anything be rational we must necessarily understand it, unless, indeed, we ourselves are irrational, a supposition not to be entertained. Nor, again, is a man's complete ignorance of the meaning of names, stories, or a subject generally, any disqualification to his treating of it at length. Has not the Unknowable itself been discussed through hundreds of pages, and shall the Unintelligible escape us? Perish the thought.

We have merely indicated the wealth of truth and learning to be found in the pages of Professor Aguchekikos, and for more must refer the eager reader to the great original. We can but just mention his interesting account of the hostile political totem tribes of the Foxes and the Wolves. How the efforts of a great ancestral Fox were said to have been stopped by a Pitt (Pit?), into which, no doubt, he fell —trapped by some early hunter; how the Anti-Foxites are reported to have sent a chieftain named Wolf to Egypt, probably to Lycopolis where, as Strabo (xvii. 40) informs us, the Wolf was worshipped, of course as a totem-ancestor; and how the transformation of men into animals, reptiles, plants, etc., which is said to be still the current creed of Cairo, Kamtchatka, and Panchoea, was fully believed in by the Britons of the Victorian Epoch, so that a man was known to say his friend had become 'a snake in the grass.' It seems, too, that there then existed a mysterious tribe of mythologists who were popularly credited with the extraordinary power of 'turning everything into the sun.' But, as for these things and many like unto them, are they not written in the pages of Aguchekikos and Driveller? A solitary sage of the time had another view about matters of the kind. He declared that religion, mythology, and belief generally were based upon dreams; and to this opinion, as one affording a good substantial foundation, we should certainly have inclined, had not the totemistic truths of the Professor dawned upon us as clear as the Aśvins. Such being the case, the dream theory, although highly commended, must fade; and we confidently predict that, notwithstanding an unworthy fear expressed in some quarters lest this key of knowledge should become as rusty as Mr. Casaubon's, the gospel according to Aguchekikos will be universally admired and adopted when Homer and Vergil are forgotten, although probably not until then.

Opinions of Some 'Allies' on Aguchekikos

'The charming' review of Totemism. I read it with intense pleasure, and wondered who the writer could be. It is as witty as it is wise, and quite a perfect work of art in its kind.'—P. Le Page Renouf.

'I was very amused by it, and it is to the point.'— Prof. C. P. Tiele (Leiden University).

'German readers will appreciate the fine humour of the little work.'—Dr. O. Gruppe (Berlin).

'Deals in the right way with one of the epidemics of nonsense with which our unfortunate nation is sick just now.' —James Anthony Froude.

'Mr. Ruskin was immensely tickled. Totemism raised inextinguishable laughter.'—W. G. COLLINGWOOD.

'Most witty.'—Dr. F. A. PALEY.

Note.—We desire to spare the blushes of the following 'Allies' :—

'An admirable burlesque upon the scientific absurdities now current.'

'Aguchekikos was beautiful. It delighted my heart.'

'The clever satire upon Totemism.'

'Very good—it hits hard.'

'I was greatly delighted with Aguchekikos.'

'The uncommon cleverness of the skit.'

'It is extremely good.'   'Splendidly effective.'

APPENDIX B

List of Papers by the Author on Astronomical Mythology

I. In the *Archaeologia*.

On a German Astronomico-Astrological Manuscript, and On the Origin of the Signs of the Zodiac, 19 illustrations (1883).

Remarks on the Gryphon, Heraldic and Mythological, 4 illustrations (1885).

'The gryphon is a worthy follower of the unicorn. You have left little more to be found out about him.'— Prof. SAYCE.

II. In the *Yorkshire Archaeological Journal*.

Remarks on the zodiacal Virgo, in connexion with a Representation of the Constellation upon the Porch of S. Margaret's Church, York, 21 illustrations (1886).

'A masterpiece.'—Prof. SAYCE.

III. In *The Babylonian and Oriental Record*.

Babylonian Astronomy in the West—the Aries of Aratos (Jan. 1887).

Remarks on some Euphratean Astronomical Names in the Lexikon of Hésychios (July-Aug. 1887).

IV. In the *Proceedings* of the Society of Biblical Archaeology.

Remarks on the Tablet of the Thirty Stars, 2 illustrations (Jan.-Feb. 1890).

Remarks on the Euphratean Astronomical Names of the Signs of the Zodiac, 18 illustrations (March, 1891).

Euphratean Stellar Researches, Part I. 5 illustrations (April, 1892), Part II. 2 illustrations (May, 1893), Part III. (June, 1893), Part IV. 5 illustrations (Jan. 1895), Part V. (Dec. 1895-Jan. 1896).

V. In the *Transactions* of the Ninth International Congress of Orientalists (London, 1892).

The Celestial Equator of Aratos. 33 illustrations.

VI. In the *Journal* of the Royal Asiatic Society.

The Origin of the Ancient Northern Constellation-figures (April, 1897).

VII. In *The Academy.*

The Early Babylonian Kings and the Ecliptic (May 31, 1884).

The Babylonian Zodiac (Jan. 29, 1887).

The Zodiacal Crab (Feb. 21, 1885 ; Dec. 6, 1890).

The Milky way in Euphratean Stellar Mythology (Jan. 9, 1892).

Soma and Rohinî (Nov. 12, 1892).

'*The Ten Patriarchs of Berosus*' (June 3, July 15, 1893).

The Te Tablet (Nov. 4, 1893).

Review of Sir Norman Lockyer's 'Dawn of Astronomy' (March 31, 1894).

The Connexion between Babylonian and Greek Astronomy (Nov. 10, 1894).

'*Fortuna Maior*' (Jan. 12, 1895).

The Archaic Lunar Zodiac (March 23, 1895).

The God Tartak (July 20, 1895).

Greek Coin Types and the Constellation Figures (Sept. 21, 1895).

Phoenicia and the Ancient Constellation Figures (Nov. 7, 1896).

INDEX

I. AUTHORS

II. GENERAL

15

www.ingramcontent.com/pod-product-compliance
Lightning Source LLC
Chambersburg PA
CBHW070403270326
41926CB00014B/2685